STAYING SOLO

Your Guide to Building
a **SIMPLE** and
SUSTAINABLE
Service Business

by Maggie Patterson
CREATOR OF BS-FREE BUSINESS

To my podcast listeners, blog readers, and most of all, my past and present BS-Free Business clients.

This book is for you. Your enthusiasm and willingness to share your stories with me for more than 10 years is why this book exists.

I'm grateful for each and every one of you.

Contents

Preface

As a writer for my entire career, you'd think that writing a book would be the most natural thing in the world for me to do. The truth is I dragged my feet on writing a book for close to 10 years.

Part of it came down to the season of life, then a bigger reason, the *real* reason... I didn't have something I felt was book-worthy yet. That is until I nailed down the concept of *staying solo*.

In late 2023, I knew it was finally time for the book, but I continued to drag my feet. After a firm push from a couple of wise friends who told me they needed this book, I decided to take the plunge.

In a way, I'm glad it has taken me this long, as the timing of this book couldn't be better. Entrepreneurship has never been more popular and there's a dramatic shift happening when it comes to how and where we work.

Running a solo service business offers a way to make a living on your own terms, yet the world is evolving rapidly. In the last five years alone, many of us have been directly impacted by a global pandemic, record inflation, questions about artificial intelligence (AI) threatening creative work, the rise of content creators, fresh new manipulative sales and marketing tactics, and so much more.

It's been a hell of a ride, and it's changed so many of us. Creating a simple, sustainable business is more important than ever.

By wanting to stay solo, you're not "playing small" as some may have you believe. You're not trying to avoid risk or act out of fear. Instead, you're choosing to build a business that's strategically small.

Having run a business for 20 years, my goal is to help you build a business that works for you as a solo business owner. One that doesn't burn you out or make you want to set it on fire. A (boring) business that's predictable, profitable and peaceful.

So screw the status quo of business. We're staying solo and doing this our way.

Making the Most of This Book

This is a book about breaking rules, so this is a reminder that you don't have to read this from start to finish to get the most out of it.

It is meant to be a guidebook, which means you can skip to whatever section is most relevant to you. Here's what you can expect in each of the three sections:

PART ONE: Is all about the broader context you're operating in as a solo service business owner. If you're the kind of person who wants to know why things are the way they are, and how we ended up at the point where the majority of business advice is generic, or completely wrong for you, definitely start here.

PART TWO: Is the heart of the book, where we dive into everything related to the Staying Solo® framework. If you want to get right into action and are already over the "scale or fail" message, and want to start working on specific aspects of your business, you may want to dive in here.

PART THREE: This is the wrap up where I explore some final questions and give you guidance on setting (and keeping) your boundaries. Plus, I share a final reminder on why bigger isn't always better and leave you with some useful resources. Everyone should read this section, but be sure to check out the guidance at the start of chapter 12.

Note: Throughout this book, I reference a number of members of my community as examples of service business owners. Their insights have been collected through questions asked on my social media channels, my annual online business survey, and personal interviews.

During my research for Staying Solo, I wanted to ensure I included a range of experiences from diverse service businesses. Among them are many experts in their field who have informed the later chapters on financials, workflows, and wellbeing for solopreneurs.

CHAPTER 1

THE NEW FACE OF ENTREPRENEURSHIP

March 13, 2020, is a day I'll never forget. I always think of it as my last "normal" day. I went to the gym and the grocery store, and prepared for what I thought would be a short break from real life thanks to COVID-19.

Little did I know what would follow would change everything, especially how we work.

Millions of people suddenly needed to work from home for the first time — something that I'd been doing since 2005 — and many of these people saw how they didn't need to be tethered to the expectations of traditional work.

The Great Resignation resulted in a record number of individuals voluntarily quitting their jobs. According to the U.S. Bureau of Labor Statistics, over 47 million Americans quit their jobs in 2021. Interestingly, this is just the continuation of a bigger trend since

2009, where the number of people leaving their jobs has increased year-over-year.

But the question is: where are these people going?

Joseph Fuller and William Kerr, Harvard Business School professors and researchers on the future of work, have coined the Five Rs to explain why people quit: retirement, relocation, reconsideration, reshuffling, and reluctance.

While retirement and relocation are clear and conclusive, reshuffling typically refers to people switching roles or sectors in order to upgrade their salary. The remaining two factors likely drive entry into entrepreneurship as an alternative to traditional work.

In the case of reconsideration, many people were forced to make drastic changes in light of the pandemic and chronic burnout.

Women in particular often had to leave their jobs to care for children as they were left with no other option, with more than two million women in the U.S. leaving during the pandemic to caretake. According to a McKinsey report, "the pandemic had a near-immediate effect on women's employment," with three groups in particular experiencing the largest challenges: working mothers, women in senior management positions, and Black women.

The ongoing lack of support for women in the workplace means that more of us are seeking out non-traditional work, and starting businesses. A study from Gusto in the US market found that almost half of startups in 2021 were formed by women, which is up from a reported 28% in 2019. Plus, Black entrepreneurs started businesses at a rate three times more than in 2019, going from 3% to 9% of total businesses.

Other individuals decided to make a move by quitting their jobs and ideally upgrading, while others left as they were reluctant to return to the office.

While not all these workers started businesses, it is clear many of them did. The U.S. Census Bureau reported that more than 4.4

million new businesses were created in the U.S. during 2020. This is the highest total on record and a 24.3% increase from 2019.

BEING SELF-EMPLOYED GOES MAINSTREAM

While entrepreneurship is nothing new, what happened in 2020 resulted in not just an influx of new business owners but a mainstream legitimization of the types of businesses many of us have been running for years.

When I started my business in 2005, it was seen as a bold move by most of my friends and family. At that time in Canada, only 15.5% of workers were self-employed.

Fast forward to 2020, and suddenly my work-from-home situation was normal. My corporate clients who had struggled over the years to understand how I didn't have a physical office no longer cared.

As of 2020, 15.18% of Americans in the workforce were self-employed, and that number has climbed steadily since then.

While entrepreneurship and being self-employed was nothing new, it felt way more mainstream in the eyes of the world at large. The definition of entrepreneurship broadened from describing someone making deals on Shark Tank or running a brick-and-mortar business, to someone like me. This is a much more accurate portrayal of entrepreneurship, as 80% of small businesses in the U.S. don't have employees, the majority of them being one-person firms with no payroll.

Yet, the teachings and tools available to most entrepreneurs are simply not designed for someone who wants to run a small, simple business as a solopreneur.

Solo business owners are often treated as if they have a cute little lifestyle business, which dismisses their skills, experience, and commitment to building something for themselves.

Venture Forward, a multiyear research project from web hosting company GoDaddy, has been actively tracking the rise of microbusinesses. The project found that fewer barriers to entry has led to a microbusiness boom. As part of this project, they've created the *Microbusiness Index* showing the impact these businesses have on the economy, with the aim of illustrating the value of even the smallest businesses.

In response to this data, Brookings Metro nonresident senior fellow Pamela D. Lewis shared that "economic development strategies may look different for microbusinesses than large businesses, requiring distinct interventions related to networking, practical assistance and mentoring."

While this highlights the major impact solo businesses have on the broader economy, the harsh reality is that they tend to be overlooked by government, financial institutions, and other organizations in favor of more traditional businesses. Coupled with the fact that solo, service-based businesses are often invisible compared to product-based businesses, or those with physical locations and a team, resources are woefully lacking.

A great example of this were the many support programs that emerged during the pandemic to help small businesses. There's no denying that brick and mortar stores were hardest hit, and there needed to be support for workers.

However, there were few programs aimed at providing support for solo, service-based business owners who in some sectors experienced a sharp decline in revenue. In Canada, programs such as the Canadian Emergency Business Account (CEBA) and the Canada Emergency Wage Subsidy (CEWS) were not accessible to solo service business owners.

There are countless examples of how solo (especially service-based) businesses are overlooked and ignored. I believe this is why it's taken to this point for people to see it as a viable career path for individuals with the right skills.

THE CULTURE OF ENTREPRENEURSHIP

When you look at entrepreneurship at the cultural level, especially in North America, it's reached a mythological status where the stories are skewed towards people who have built massive, incredibly successful businesses.

A great example of this type of entrepreneurship are the "sharks" on Shark Tank, such as Barbara Corcoran (net worth: $100 million), Mark Cuban (net worth: $6.86 billion), and Daymond John (net worth: $350 million).

Then, there are the new crop of "self-made" entrepreneurs and influencers all over TikTok, Instagram, and YouTube that focus heavily on selling a glossy and highly curated image of their luxury lives, thanks to the money they earn from their digital presence. They flaunt the trappings of wealth as proof of their skill, expertise, and most of all their success.

This is not the reality of entrepreneurship for most people, and research into the landscape of entrepreneurship tells a very different story:

- Average annual revenue for non-employer firms in the US is $46,978.
- Less than 2% of single-person businesses become millionaires.
- When it comes to small business owner salaries, 86.3% of

small business owners said they take a yearly salary of less than $100,000.

THE BUSINESS OF ENTREPRENEURSHIP

A particularly compelling piece of research is: *Towards an Untrepreneurial Economy? The Entrepreneurship Industry and the Rise of the Veblenian Entrepreneur* by Hartmann, Spicer and Krabbe (2019). This paper explores how an entire industry has been created around the ideology of entrepreneurialism.

The paper details how, in the industry of entrepreneurship, there are countless products created and marketed as a form of conspicuous consumption. Products are "focused on encouraging and supporting the pursuit of entrepreneurial opportunities by providing goods and services specifically for entrepreneurs."

This ideology and industry make it socially acceptable to "start businesses and get rich from doing so," and engage in what has been called a "one-sided cultural celebration of entrepreneurs" (from Jones and Spicer in their 2009 book, *Unmasking the Entrepreneur*).

Hartmann and associates' research introduces us to the concept of the *Veblenian Entrepreneur*, or *wantrepreneur*. Thorstein Veblen was an economist and sociologist who coined the term *conspicuous consumption*, a phrase used to describe the practice of consumers purchasing to signal status or display wealth.

Entrepreneurs consuming the products of this industry should be considered Veblenian as they're "driven primarily by the desire to build the identity of an entrepreneur." The idea is that it's socially attractive to be an entrepreneur.

However, we need to acknowledge the level of privilege and resources required to be able to make these purchases and invest this time into the pursuit of entrepreneurship. This is backed up by research from Bell and their colleagues (2018), as well as Marinoni and Voorheis (2019). Their research shows how "gains from an entrepreneurial activity are concentrated in the top of income distribution, implying a broader picture of unequal chances of entrepreneurial success."

In other words, when entrepreneurship is glamorized for financial gain, it has a harmful impact on those less able to achieve it in the first place.

THE REALITY OF ENTREPRENEURIAL FAILURE

In 2010, Hayward and others shared a paper titled *Beyond Hubris: How Highly Confident Entrepreneurs Rebound to Venture Again*, which is shared in the Hartmann research. It reports that positive results are "picked out and given significantly more emphasis than more negative information."

The truth is that in this industry, on the whole, outcomes are skewed. In many ways, we're being sold this idea that entrepreneurship will be fulfilling and help us reach our goals, when really it's about convincing us to buy something.

This ties in with what's called Survivorship Bias, which according to DecisionLab is a "cognitive shortcut that occurs when a visible, successful subgroup is mistaken as an entire group, due to the failure subgroup not being visible."

We don't see the failures, so we think we're going to be super successful. And the industry of entrepreneurship perpetuates this with its storytelling and use of testimonials.

Hamilton's findings were stark when discussing failure in the 2020 paper titled *Does Entrepreneurship Pay?* One finding in particular really stood out to me: that "entrepreneurs have lower lifetime earnings than wage earners."

A 2023 Report from the US Bureau of Labor Statistics (BLS) found that 20.8% of businesses fail within the first year. Additional BLS data found that by the end of year two 30% will have failed, and by the end of year five approximately 50% will have failed. Fast forward a decade and only 30% will remain.

There are countless reasons why businesses fail and it's worth noting that any dissolution of a business is counted as a failure in the eyes of BLS. Some of this data is, therefore, unlikely to mean failure in the sense we are talking about for self-employed service businesses.

However, in my experience, service business owners typically shut up shop/close their doors/give up on entrepreneurship when they don't find enough clients. That may be due to lack of service demand, inadequate marketing, or poor client delivery. Regardless of the reason, nothing will sink a solo service business faster than a lack of consistent revenue.

I don't share these numbers because I think owning a business is a terrible idea and you're doomed to fail. Instead, I want to drive home the point that starting and running a business is much, much harder than this culture of entrepreneurship leads us to believe.

It's a far cry from the widespread celebration of entrepreneurship within Western culture, and the relentless "make millions" message we're inundated with online.

The industry of entrepreneurship has a vested interest in convincing us that starting a business is relatively easy, which often leads to unrealistic expectations. Thankfully, there's a middle ground between these false promises and abject failure.

PERSIST OR PACK IT IN?

As someone who's had a business in one form or another for 20 years, I've watched hundreds of my peers come and go. They start businesses then life changes, or maybe they just need a different type of way to support themselves. On the other hand, they may simply discover that entrepreneurship isn't everything it's cracked up to be.

One of the hardest (yet bravest) things entrepreneurs can do is walk away from their business. Often, any change in status is immediately chalked up as a failure. However, in my mind, doing what's best for you in any given season is a success that should be celebrated.

After all, isn't that the reason why so many of us start businesses in the first place? Do we want more freedom and agency over how we live our lives, or do we want to be doing something that's dragging us down and making us miserable?

Hartmann and associates discuss a situation I've seen too many times to count, which they termed "persistence regardless of performance." Essentially, this is where business owners are so bound and determined that they're going to make things work despite what their results say that they invest an escalating amount of time and money into their venture.

This is a prime example of Sunk Cost Fallacy at play. The Oxford Dictionary defines this as "the phenomenon whereby a person is reluctant to abandon a strategy or course of action because they have invested heavily in it, even when it is clear that abandonment would be more beneficial."

The research by Hartmann and associates found that when people perform poorly, they think they need more support and more products. Then, they keep consuming more and more products and services because they think they should be able to make things work. (And for the people selling these offers, this works for them as it helps increase their bottom line.)

For you to thrive as a business owner, especially one who wants to stay solo, you need to fully understand that this shit is hard. There is no easy button and sometimes the best possible decision is knowing when to tap out.

Of course, it's not always about throwing good money after bad. With the correct instruction or simply a more favorable economic environment, yes, persisting could be the correct course. But first a word on where to get your information.

BAD BUSINESS ADVICE ABOUNDS

The current state of the internet means there is a 24/7 influx of opinions from anyone with access to a Wi-Fi connection. While there's a distinct upside to the democratization of information, the downside is that people who are anything but experts can masquerade as such on the internet.

On the podcast I co-host with my friend, Dr. Michelle Mazur, called *Duped: The Dark Side of Online Business*, we've termed these bullshit artists "faux experts." These individuals build entire businesses by claiming expertise they don't actually have.

A good example of this in action is the case of Texas-based influencer Brittany Dawn Davis, a fitness influencer who was sued by the State of Texas for alleged deceptive business practices.

Between 2014 and 2019, Davis sold fitness and nutrition plans ranging from $92 to $300, and was sued for non-delivery. She'd built a large Instagram following by sharing her journey of recovery from an eating disorder; however, she had no formal training in fitness or nutrition.

The lawsuit says Davis provided generic and non-substantive feedback, such as "you're killing it" and "you've got this babe!"

Before the trial began in May 2023, she ended up settling with the State of Texas, agreeing to pay $300,000 in civil penalties and $100,000 in restitution, with both amounts due within three years. Additionally, Davis is prohibited from claiming that she has special training or knowledge related to eating disorders.

While Davis is a fitness influencer, this is a very public example of a scenario I see daily with business advice. We have business coaches who know nothing about business teaching people how to start a business or how to be a business coach.

Author Michael Lewis covered expertise in season three of the *Against the Rules* podcast, exploring why true experts often struggle to be recognized as such. Through a series of stories, he illustrates how they struggle to communicate and promote their message.

Dr. Michelle Mazur, whose work is dedicated to helping professionals become known for their work, refers to these individuals as "overlooked experts." This is necessary and important work, especially in the realm of entrepreneurship.

Becoming known isn't about being internet famous or having millions of followers. It's really about mastering your craft and being respected for the work you do. I'll be sharing stories throughout *Staying Solo*® of people who've done exactly that as solo business owners.

However, the culture around entrepreneurship results in what Hartmann and colleagues deem an emphasis on "characteristics like overconfidence, risk tolerance and optimism."

The result is that we can too easily take advice from faux experts, doing ourselves and our businesses a major disservice.

I asked members of my community to share stories about "bad" advice that negatively impacted their business. Here's just a sample of the advice they received.

"The reason you feel imposter syndrome isn't because you need training to become a coach. You just need to be one step ahead of your clients."

"Never charge by the hour."

"You have anxiety because you're misaligned with your true mission."

"Just add a zero to your pricing. Just triple your prices. Someone out there is willing to pay."

"I was told I needed to hire to expand my business. I ended up with a business partner under the impression it was necessary to grow."

At a glance, these recommendations may not seem problematic; however, the reality is that we need individualized advice that's suitable for our own business model. These suggestions are shallow and not suitable for everyone. Yet, this is the nature of most advice offered in the online business world on a day-to-day basis.

As nutrition therapist and certified intuitive eating counsellor Sarah Berneche notes: "Apart from the financial cost, much of the advice I received was out of alignment with my values and prioritized revenue over client service."

WHEN BUSINESS ADVICE TURNS TOXIC

As humans, we're hardwired to overestimate our competence and place too much faith in our intuition. This default setting, coupled with the fact that we can't automatically trust the source of the information (or what we're learning from it) and that it might not be specific to our situation, creates a recipe for potential problems.

For years, I've watched well-meaning business owners default to generalized advice from a random podcaster they've never met, instead of listening to wise counsel from people who know the ins and outs of their business. These people want to believe in the dream being sold to them and completely overlook the realities of what they really need in their business.

This is where advice culture can become toxic, as not all advice is created equal. There's a major difference between the in-depth guidance you'll get from a coach, consultant, or mentor, and the one-size-fits-all teachings of a YouTuber or podcaster.

Each of us needs to carefully discern what advice is right for us and our business. This is especially important as the faux-expert industry thrives on deception and manipulation to ensnare even the savviest consumers. They package their "expertise" into appealing products that waste our time, money, and energy — but we often don't realize this until it's too late.

As coach Diann Wingert reflects on her experiences: "There have been a number of times, but the common denominator is that in each case, the advice was generic, one-size-fits-all ('it worked for me and it will work for you'), and usually included phrases like 'my proven process' and 'step by step guidance.' It still shocks me that I was so willing to hand over large sums of money to these shamelessly self-promoting internet gurus when I started my online coaching business, especially after I had already launched and run a very successful psychotherapy practice for a number of years."

BUILDING A SERVICES BUSINESS IS HARDER THAN IT LOOKS

As entrepreneurship has become more and more common, there's a misalignment between its mainstream media image and the realities we face as business owners. Most businesses are one-person businesses, yet conventional teachings about building a business are focused on strategies unsuitable for solopreneurs. This is complicated by the fact that faux experts are everywhere online, dispensing generalized advice that can easily derail your business.

In the next chapter, you'll see just how growing a solo service-based business requires us to act in accordance with our values and prioritize sustainability.

CHAPTER 2

SCALE OR SUSTAINABILITY?

The dominant narrative about business growth is that you need to be focused on scaling, or you're somehow failing.

Scaling your business is seen as the ultimate goal for every business owner. As a result, business coaching, books, courses, podcasts, and articles focus heavily on how to grow your business rapidly.

This is some of the most toxic and frankly unhelpful advice for service business owners, particularly those who have no desire to build a team, or don't know that building a team isn't for them as they've never done it before.

"Scale" is a buzzword that's become shorthand for growth. The idea is that you should scale your business in order to increase your revenue and ultimately your profits.

The reality is that growing a business is *not* the same as scaling a business. Growing a business means adding revenue, but may also entail adding expenses. Improving income by $20k and then adding team costs of $20k may drive growth, but this isn't true scale.

Increasing revenue is growth, not scale, despite how it's discussed by celebrity entrepreneurs (my pet name for business coaches and influencers who "teach us" how to do business).

These coaches and consultants use the word scale as a way to talk about offers, marketing, and tech that will help you grow, typically to multiple six or even seven figures. The result is that the promise of scale and building a million-dollar-plus business is oversold.

If you pay careful attention to how these businesses are being built, you'll see how they tend to hire more and more people as they increase revenue, with their marketing costs also rising exponentially.

The real goal of scaling is to increase revenue while also driving efficiency. To effectively scale, you need to build the foundations in order to support growth.

According to SCORE, a non-profit designed to provide free advice to small businesses in the US, to scale, you need "planning, some funding, and the right systems, staff, processes, technology, and partners."

Growth and scale are very different. For the majority of businesses, particularly service businesses, focusing on scaling can result in major structural issues and cash flow problems.

The book *Scaling Up* by Verne Harnish, a respected expert on scaling up businesses, details just how hard it is for businesses to grow and how few companies get past the million dollar mark. When the book was written in 2014, of the "roughly 28 million companies in the US, only 4% make it to generating $1 million in revenue per year."

Harnish discusses a phenomenon called the "valley of death," where at certain revenue milestones there's a danger zone that the company must travel through. One of Harnish's revenue milestones where you enter the valley of death as you scale is at the million dollar mark.

The lesson? Scale is often a far cry from the growth trajectory promised.

THE CULT OF SCALE

This is where what I call "the cult of scale" comes in. We're constantly sold the idea that being successful depends on our ability to scale.

We're indoctrinated by a specific version of success that comes in the form of building our personal wealth and hitting big revenue numbers.

In many cases, the tactics used to sell us the dream of scaling our businesses are troubling as they're about conditioning us into a certain way of thinking and behaving. The goal is to get us to believe it's possible for us too, so we'll buy a product or service such as coaching or pay for advice from a high-ticket mastermind.

The result is that scale is seen as the righteous path and anything less means you're playing small. Scaling your business and focusing on ever-increasing revenue milestones is viewed as 'The Thing' to do.

Over the years, I've had countless conversations with clients where they express their feelings of "doing something wrong" as they're not interested in "going all in" by scaling their business.

They aren't willing to subscribe to the idea that they should aggressively grow their business just so they don't feel like an outsider or simply to fit in.

While the cult of scale isn't a cult in the traditional sense, the parallels are there. As Amanda Montell shares in her book *Cultish*, many groups and everyday things can be cult-like and no one is immune to their power.

For some of you, terming this a "cult" may be a bit of an over-reach, but what seals the deal for me is the willingness of many businesses (especially the online-based personality-driven brands) to use high-pressure, cult-like tactics to achieve scale.

While many of these tactics, from "handling objections" to using emotional manipulation and insider secrets, are extremely common in online business, they're also right out of Dr. Steven Hassan's BITE Model.

If you're unfamiliar with Dr. Hassan's work, he is an expert on cults and undue influence. The BITE acronym stands for Behavior, Information, Thought, and Emotional Control. If you review the BITE Model in detail, you'll quickly see that many of the teachings and tactics around scaling and running a business taught by online personalities are more cult-like than most of us realize.

When you look critically at how, as entrepreneurs, we're taught to scale our businesses and the methods to do so, it's very clear that the cult of scale is really about worshipping at the altar of capitalism (probably the biggest cult to which we all belong) — even if it's dressed up as being about changing the world or "women's wealth."

WHEN SCALING IS HARMFUL, NOT HELPFUL

This narrative, and the wider cultural celebration of business growth, does a massive con job on all of us as it attempts to convince us that scaling our business is about more than acquiring wealth.

FACTS: Capitalism, by any other name, is still capitalism.

As bell hooks writes in *Feminist Theory: From Margins to Center,* much of the current approach to feminism is rooted in the idea that women acquire "wealth and power as a prerequisite to feminist struggle."

That's exactly what happens every day among business owners. When you focus on scaling as a means to get "free," you're simply buying into the extractive nature of our capitalist system.

Listen, I'm the first to say that you need to make money to pay the bills; ignoring your financial needs is not what I'm talking about here. What I'm referring to is this idea that by scaling your business you're automatically going to make the world a better place.

As a consultant, the majority of the solo business owners I work with are women. And as women, one of the most prevalent messages we're fed is that we should be chasing a big revenue goal. The idea is that when we make more money, we'll make the world a better place.

This type of financial feminism uses the logic of trickle-down economics, that is, the idea that women acquiring wealth "trickles" down to other women. As brand and business strategist Susana Baker said to me, "It's trickle-down economics but in pink."

In many ways, the message of financial feminism within entrepreneurship weaponizes our lack of financial literacy and manipulates us into thinking our businesses need to be the vehicle for change.

Honestly, that's a metric shitload of pressure, particularly in the current climate. So many people are simply trying to survive right now, and it's no small feat to "change the world" by building your business.

By no means am I writing a permission slip for us all to check out and stop caring about what's happening around us. Instead, I ask: Why does our business need to be the vehicle for paying the bills *and* having personal fulfilment *and* living out our purpose *and* having like-minded friends *and* contributing to the community *and* doing good *and* leaving a legacy *and* changing the world?

Sounds like a lot of bullshit to me because it places a lot of pressure and unrealistic expectations on your business to be the be-all-and-end-all. Honestly, it's a story created by celebrity entrepreneurs to make your business your entire identity and world so you'll pay for their programs.

Let's dial that back to doing what you can on a day-to-day basis and more importantly, not falling for the BS lie of "scale your business no matter what" that requires you to exploit yourself, your clients, your team, and more to achieve your goals.

After all, what good is your donation to a political campaign because you hit a revenue milestone when you've worked yourself into a state of complete burnout while price-gouging your clients?

This is where scale is harmful, not helpful. It sounds appealing for so many reasons, but scale often comes at a steep cost.

On a personal level, as you scale, it's easy to fall into a cycle of endless hustling. Chasing scale is closely aligned with the tenets of hustle culture — the idea that you should always be working hard in order to be "successful" and that your worth is measured through the accumulation of fame, power, and wealth.

It's important to remember that hustle culture is the natural extension of the American Dream, where we're taught that if we work hard, we'll become rich. Of course, riches are not a foregone conclusion just because someone works hard; and most of all in business where results are not guaranteed by effort.

Chasing the dream or doggedly pursuing a certain lifestyle can have hugely detrimental effects, not only on the business's bottom line but on a business owner's health too.

Entrepreneurs are particularly susceptible to the downsides of hustle culture. Brittany Berger from Work Brighter, a digital media company committed to a version of productivity that makes room for "unproductive" things like rest, self-care, and fun, has written and spoken extensively about how hustle culture impacts entrepreneurship:

"The entrepreneurship and the online business community really take hustle culture up a notch from its already intense levels. I think the people who are most into hustle culture in the first place are the same people who get drawn to online business and entrepreneurship. So, it's just like a sampling bias in one way, which results in being susceptible to burnout due to work habits."

BUILDING ON THE BACKS OF UNDERPAID AND OVERWORKED TEAMS

Conventional business teachings about scale often focus heavily on hiring a team and maximizing profits at all costs. As someone who's done their fair share of hiring, I have zero issue with growing a business and building a team to work alongside you.

What is objectionable is how people treat and pay their teams.

The overwhelming focus of conversations about hiring, especially in the online business space, are about freeing up the business owner so they can leverage their time. On the surface, there's nothing wrong with that as the business owner's skills and energy need to be on the highest value tasks.

Where this goes completely off the rails is that most of the people I see providing this advice are concerned about one thing and one thing only, and that's building their personal wealth.

Scale happens on the backs of their teams who may be underpaid and overworked.

A quick review on Glassdoor of the online-based coaching and education companies pushing this message to solo and microbusinesses reveals the ruthless reality of how these companies are run, and how they're reaching those big revenue goals.

Employees share their experiences of what these companies are really like on the inside using words such as "volatile," "abusive," and "toxic." To paraphrase one review, employees are kept in fear, manipulated, and subject to intolerable work conditions.

There's no denying these conditions exist in corporate settings, but the stark difference is that the majority of these companies claim to empower women and other marginalized groups, while actually exploiting them.

Beyond the treatment, there's the issue of compensation.

It's not just teams that are being exploited. Customers are often being taken advantage of as pricing rises exponentially. A brief look at the price of services of online-based business coaches clearly illustrates this point. Pricing for an hour of coaching can be anywhere from $100 an hour to over $10,000. Ongoing coaching can be as much as $50,000 or more for six months.

This may seem extreme, but it's increasingly common online as people realize they can charge exorbitant prices and there will be people willing to pay. As much as I'd like to dismiss this as being between the coach and their client, the truth is that highly manipulative marketing and sales practices (such as high-pressure phone calls, false scarcity, unrepresentative testimonials, and hugely marked up payment plans to name a few) are being used to scale the company, and ultimately grow their personal net worth.

Scaling this way does considerable harm to the business owner, their team, and their client.

So, if you don't want to be one of those kinds of businesses, you don't want to scale this way, and actually want to stay solo as a business owner, is that a viable path?

The answer is yes. There is another way, and that's at the heart of the remainder of this book.

SHEDDING BULLSHIT EXPECTATIONS

Given that *Staying Solo* is designed to be the antidote to this unsustainable path to business growth, what does that look like?

It means more and more business owners are rejecting this broken blueprint as they're not interested in hustling and exploiting their way to a bullshit version of success.

I'm going to hazard a guess you're one of those business owners.

In my experience, the siren call of doing business in a way that's about power, fame, and wealth is treated as the norm, and it takes courage and commitment to diverge from the status quo of entrepreneurship.

One of the biggest lessons we can all learn from businesses that fail is that it's often because they skipped the fundamentals and literally broke their businesses.

I get it. The fundamentals aren't always flashy or exciting, but they're the secret sauce behind my clients who are thriving in their businesses. They run relatively drama-free, boring ass businesses that get them paid.

Think of it this way. Would you rather hit a big revenue milestone once and then have to close your doors because you're so burnt out that you can't keep going?

Or would you rather build something more slowly that you can sustain for five, ten, or more years? Would you rather your business pay you well and let you do things other than work all the damn time?

I know what I'd rather choose, and unsubscribing from the cult of scale is the way to build something that endures — a business that's both simple and truly sustainable.

WHAT IS BUSINESS SUSTAINABILITY?

As someone who's been running my own business for 20 years, sustainability has always been my top priority. I'm more interested in having a business 10 years from now and supporting my lifestyle than sacrificing my values to reach a vanity metric related to revenue or the number of followers I have.

Side note: I want to acknowledge that I hold many privileges which have made that possible. There's no way I would have been able to start my business without the stability of my partner's career, and as a white, cis, het, able-bodied, university-educated Canadian, I had many advantages right out of the gate.

What does it really mean to have a "sustainable" business? How can we build something that's truly sustainable?

It's important to note that sustainability is not a new concept; it should be recognized as central to the values and teachings of North American Indigenous peoples. As Rebecca Tsosie, a senior sustainability scientist and Regent's Professor of Law at Arizona State University, writes, "Indigenous peoples have survived as separate and distinct nations within often-challenging natural, political and economic environments precisely because they maintain cultural values consistent with sustainability."

At the heart of sustainability is recognizing that resources are finite, and that we need to act accordingly. The UN World Commission on Environment and Development defines sustainable development as "development that meets the needs of the present without compromising the ability of future generations to meet their own needs."

Usually, sustainability is thought of in terms of climate change and environmental practices, but in the Brundtland Report the

United Nations identifies the three pillars of sustainability as being the environment, economy, and society. The idea is that any organization must contribute to "economic growth, social progress and promote environmental sustainability."

For solo business owners, you have the ability to make choices that balance your actions today with the needs of the future. Admittedly, this can prove to be particularly challenging as pursuing short-term gains — such as saying yes to a questionable but lucrative client — has a direct impact on our personal compensation.

Ultimately, to have a business that's truly sustainable you need to realize that you're a finite resource. You can't do the work you're meant to do if you're constantly hustling and engaging in business practices that have a negative impact.

Sustainability is a specific approach to running your business and may require you to make decisions that go against traditional teachings of entrepreneurship. The purpose of Staying Solo® is to help you get to a point where your business is sustainable and simple as a minimum standard.

Ideally, your business would be regenerative, meaning you're creating "positive impacts on the environment, society and economy." I use the word "ideally" here on purpose, as the majority of solo business owners are trapped in the entrepreneurship industrial complex and getting to true sustainability would be a major win.

Having a sustainable business strategy requires that you untether from the status quo of business, from the cult of scale, and from capitalism, and consider how you can run your business in a way that's not extractive or exploitative.

The real secret of sustainability is that there are no shortcuts or secrets to building a business, despite what the industry of entrepreneurship may claim.

SUSTAINABILITY AS A SOLO BUSINESS OWNER

As a solo business owner, you have limited resources. Prioritizing sustainability forces you to be a good steward of those resources while respecting the environment, economy, and society at large. Plus, it's a tangible way to ensure you're running a business in alignment with your values.

This approach to your business has a significant impact on you as an individual, as well as your clients, and by extension your communities and society as a whole.

In thinking about sustainability in the context of your business, a missing piece of the puzzle can be a strategic decision not to grow any further and to simply sustain what you've built.

No one really talks about this, but it's okay to grow slowly or to stay where you are. You don't need to hire a team or grow your revenue every single year. The beauty of Staying Solo as a business owner is that you can choose based on what works best for you.

Remember Vern Harnish's Valley of Death where businesses struggle to reach the next revenue level? In my experience, there are several valleys of death for microbusinesses, or as I call them "revenue breakpoints" that naturally happen before the million-dollar mark.

A common one is at the $100k mark, another is at the $250k mark, and another is at the $500k mark. The exact numbers here may vary, but at each stage you'll need to make significant investments to make it to the next level.

When looking at what it may take to get through that next revenue breakpoint, you need to consider if that's a sustainable decision for you and your business.

For example, let's say you're at $150,000 in revenue and feeling like you're stalled out. Conventional wisdom here would be that you need to hire and possibly shift towards an agency business model. That makes the assumption that you want to have a team or run an agency, which is not the case for the majority of business owners.

Hiring is resource-intensive, and you'll need to invest time, money, and energy into your hire for months before you're in a position to generate more revenue. To go from $150,000 to $200,000 in annual revenue, you'll need to be ready for a lag effect and a possible hit to your profit in the meantime.

Hiring is just one solution though. For someone who wants to stay solo, there are other less resource-intensive — and frankly lower-risk — ways to make the jump from $150,000 to $200,000 a year.

This shows how the most common decision isn't always the right one for you, or necessarily the most sustainable one.

You have many more options than you may realize to grow and sustain your business, especially as a solopreneur. I wrote this book to provide you with fresh ideas and inspiration on exactly how to do that so you can have a simple, sustainable business.

What you do with those ideas is up to you.

All of this is a personal decision you get to make as the leader of your business based on your specific situation. That said, it shouldn't be motivated purely by a revenue goal. You need to look at the full picture including what's needed to grow, and how you can ensure what you're doing is truly sustainable.

Chapter 3

STAYING SOLO®

A Viable Path to a Sustainable Business

For nine years, I've been mentoring and consulting with owners of various sized service-based businesses. This has provided me with an inside look at what really goes on behind the scenes, as well as the highs and lows faced by these entrepreneurs.

Most of my clients and community are solo business owners. Something I've heard time and time again is that these business owners really don't want to grow an agency. They don't want to scale. They don't want to grow a million-dollar business.

Yet, they see very few examples of how exactly to stay solo, especially if they're an established business owner with the basics handled. Within many entrepreneurial circles, especially in the online business ecosystem, if you don't want to commit to chasing 7- or 8-figure revenue goals, you're accused of playing small.

If you're not familiar with the concept of playing small, it means you're choosing not to live up to your potential and that you have a mindset block in your way.

This line of thinking is extremely flawed as there's zero recognition of the fact that many people start businesses motivated by factors other than accumulating wealth.

Data from the U.S. Census Bureau found that wanting to make more money was the top motivation in 14 states. In the remaining 36 states the top reasons included:

- A flexible schedule
- Balanced life and work
- The best avenue for ideas
- Couldn't find a job
- Be my own boss
- Help my community

When you consider these reasons, it's clear that the underlying motivation isn't always about money, but often, a desire to have the flexibility and control to live life in a different way.

This is what's called a lifestyle business, where the founder has built a business based on their skills so that they can prioritize their life over working. The business is designed to support the type of life you want to create.

The word "lifestyle" may conjure up images of people flying on private jets to luxury destinations, but it's actually more about being able to earn a living while focusing on what's important to you.

In my case, I started my business purely so I wouldn't have to commute nearly two hours a day once I had my son. With a partner who worked shifts and the fact I travelled frequently for work, I didn't see a way to have the life I wanted and stay in my then role.

My story is the story of so many people who decide to start their own solo service business.

Tressa Beheim, who's an online business manager, started her business after moving to Germany for her husband's work. With two kids, and a six-hour time difference with the United States, she needed the flexibility to work completely remotely. At the time, remote work wasn't as common as it is now. Tressa told me, "I needed far more control over my hours and responsibilities than is typical for an employee."

Content writer Emily Gertenbach found herself at a breaking point — leading her to starting her business: "I simply couldn't stick it out anymore. I tried, but I was exhausted from navigating a workplace where I had to be on the defensive to protect myself physically, emotionally and professionally. I decided my mental health was worth the financial risk."

Marlene Oliveira, a non-profit communications consultant, found herself burnt out and knowing that her existing role had run its course: "I didn't think I'd be happier in a similar role at a different organization. With the encouragement of both my colleagues and my boss at the time, I decided to test my entrepreneurial mettle and try consulting."

"I didn't want to be stuck in corporate," explains Lee Densmer, a content marketer. "I wanted the freedom to do what I please, for whom I please, and not to have to do work I'm not good at or don't like. I love what I do, and now I love it more because I'm doing it on my own terms."

When I asked my community this question, only a small fraction even mentioned the money.

Why then is the narrative around entrepreneurship so heavily skewed towards talking about the money?

Maybe it's the fact we live in a capitalist system, or that the people most visible in the industry are obsessed with traditional measures of success, that means we can't seem to shake this narrative.

Businesses with lifestyle as the central motivation are just as valid as businesses that exclusively chase profits. And there's no magic revenue number that qualifies anyone as a more "legit" business owner than anyone else.

You're not playing small by staying solo. You're choosing a specific type of business that's smart and strategic. It's a choice based on how you want to run your business and what matters to you.

This book gives you a foundation to build a service business that works for you as a team of one. A business that serves you. A business that lasts.

MYTHS ABOUT STAYING SOLO AS A SERVICE BUSINESS OWNER

Now, let's tackle a few myths that I often hear from people regarding the choice to stay solo. I hear these often from people who aren't wholly convinced that they can actually remain as a team of one and still reach their goals.

As I described in chapter 1, it's worth noting that many of the myths about staying solo and running a service business are the result of years of marketing done by people selling you products and services to help you grow your business. They have a vested interest in perpetuating these myths as they create fear, uncertainty, and doubt that can compel you to buy their books, programs, coaching services and courses.

The industry of entrepreneurship weaponizes and then monetizes your desire to succeed. Always remember that when you're all up in your head, feeling like your business totally sucks or that you're doing it all wrong.

None of it is true. NONE OF IT.

Just a few of the pervasive myths about solo and service businesses that are total and complete bullshit include:

Myth: Your Income is Capped.

Reality: Solo business owners have many options to increase their revenue, from pricing to selling strategy to serving different clientele.

Myth: You Need a Team, or You'll Burn Out.

Reality: Burnout isn't inevitable as a solo business owner. Having a team is not an insurance policy against burning out.

Myth: You Have to Invest Big Bucks to Be in the Room.

Reality: While you need support as you grow a business, you don't need to pay $25k to be in a program or community.

Myth: You Need to Stop Trading Time for Dollars.

Reality: Work is trading time for dollars, any way you slice it. And let's be real; these celeb entrepreneurs are working their booties off and exploiting their teams to make bank.

Myth: You Need to Follow XYZ Formula.

Reality: There's no one way to build your business; not every approach will work for you. This is why I'm a huge fan of individualization and recognizing that we're all unique in how we approach our businesses.

Myth: Your Mindset is Holding You Back.

Reality: Not everything is a mindset issue. Seriously. These people are out here preying on us by telling us we're not good enough. No more of that, thank you very much.

This book shatters these myths and shows you how to look past trending business advice to find real, sound business wisdom. Wisdom that says you know what's best regarding your business.

That's not to say you don't need certain foundations in place, but rather that you need to discern when something is an actual challenge and when it's just an idea planted in your psyche by someone trying to sell their magical solution.

Within the online business space in particular, there's one final myth that I've encountered repeatedly: a misguided idea that if you're running a solo business, you're not a "real" business.

FACTS: Most Businesses are Solo Businesses

Remember, 80% of businesses in the U.S. are sole proprietors. Staying solo is hardly a radical choice when it describes the majority of business owners, yet solo business owners are treated as though they're failing.

This is exactly why we need to focus on practical ways for business owners to stay solo, and why I've created a six-pillar framework to help you do just that.

Over the last two to three years, I've recognized that solo business owners need a way to acknowledge the need for foundational elements, and the flexibility to decide what a simple and sustainable business looks like for them.

THE STAYING SOLO® FRAMEWORK

This is why I created the Staying Solo® Framework. There's a major gap in the market between basic business education and teaching focused only on relentless scale.

Through my work with solo, service-based business owners, I've identified a number of places where they get stuck. They find themselves working in a way that's preventing them from progressing how they'd like in their business or living the type of life they'd envisioned when they started.

The Staying Solo® Framework is designed to provide a guide to addressing these specific, foundational requirements for solo business owners, while avoiding overly prescriptive advice that ignores the nuances of your individual situation.

You always get to choose how, what, and when you do things in your business. That's the damn point of being your own boss, and I believe to the very core of my being that you're the foremost expert on you.

In the subsequent chapters of this book, I'll be diving into each of the six pillars of Staying Solo in more detail, but I want to share them all now so you know what to expect.

Salary: Getting You Paid

You started a business to make money, so your salary should be the cornerstone of your business. In this context, I'm referring to setting a personal salary goal and using that to plan your finances, pricing, expenses, and more.

Space: Creating Capacity

For you to stay solo (and not drive yourself into the ground), you need space. Space comes in many forms, including working on the business (doing things other than client work, from marketing to finances) and not just in it, as well as time away from the business.

Learning to manage your space is an essential skill as your time, and your emotional and energetic capacity, are limited.

Strategy: Breaking the Income Ceiling

Often, a solo business owner's biggest challenge is hitting an income ceiling. While pricing is a factor in making more money, strategy is our most powerful lever.

Strategy refers to both selling strategy to your clients (so you can command more cash and position yourself as a true expert) and your overall business strategy.

Support: Gathering Your Squad

Being a solo business owner doesn't mean you're doing it alone. You support your clients, but you need support too.

Support comes in many forms from professionals who support you in your business (or life), coaching or consulting, to a community of people who get it.

Systems: Ditching Busywork

As a team of one, you need ways to maximize your time and cut the busywork. Simple systems (that you actually use) supporting you with your marketing, sales and service, are essential.

Seasons: Planning Practically

A big reason you started a business is flexibility, yet it's easy to work too much and get trapped in a cycle of hustling when you're solo. Seasons are about adjusting to the natural cycles in your business, not using arbitrary dates on a calendar; it's about developing a realistic planning process that works for you, not against you.

If at any point you're feeling uncomfortable with what I'm sharing, I'm going to challenge you to stop and consider that there may be a reason for that.

I tend to be extremely stubborn when I'm first confronted with what I know to be true. I always need some time to process it and arrive at a conclusion on my terms. You may be the same.

The questions I encourage you to consider with each pillar in the 6-step framework are:

- How is this REALLY going for me right now?
- How would things change if I did this differently?
- What can I implement in my business to make my life easier?

BREAKING DOWN THE FRAMEWORK FURTHER

Now, let's dig into each of these pillars in detail. Keep in mind as you read through each of these sections that some of them may resonate with you more than others, and that's exactly the point. Different pillars will be more relevant to you at different times in your journey as a service business owner.

Also, resist the urge to start tinkering with multiple areas of your business all at once. When the goal is to run a sustainable business, you're unsubscribing from false urgency, and you can implement changes at the pace that works for you.

Finally, if at any point you feel overwhelmed and stuck on the "how" of making any of this happen, don't worry — I've got you covered. Towards the end of the book, we're going to talk about the critical role of boundaries and consistency in being able to actually *do* everything I'm sharing.

Chapter 4

Getting Your Salary Paid First

Too many solo business owners are underpaid (or not paid at all) as they fall into the trap of overinvesting in the business or pricing their services too low. And I'm not here for it.

In this chapter, we're looking at the nuts and bolts of paying yourself a salary as a solo business owner.

One of my favorite things about running a service business is how little investment you need to get started. While you need a little more than I did when I started in 2005 with some business cards and a used laptop, the simplicity of a service business is that you don't need a lot of extras.

You can run a service business with minimal expenses to retain your revenue.

When I was starting out as a solo business owner, my expenses were typically 30% of my revenue. The remaining 70% would go towards my salary and taxes. The more entrenched I became in the online business world and the industry of entrepreneurship, the more my profit margin was eroded by needless expenses I felt I needed to absorb.

Most of those needless expenses were the result of really good marketing that made me feel like I was missing something. Despite being a seasoned business owner, the constant drumbeat of unsolicited messages around how to do business better, better, better, wore me down. As a result, I invested in coaches, courses, and programs as a way to fill that gap.

Between 2013 and 2018, I made 12 significant investments with a total price tag of $72,700 USD.

Of those 12 investments, I consider three of them a success as they created direct return on investment (ROI) by helping me reach specific goals. Another three from my list I can attribute indirect ROI to from relationships I built or skills development.

All in, that's a 50% success rate. Meanwhile, the other 50% of so-called investments eroded my time, energy, and profit margin.

I quickly caught on to what was happening and adjusted my expenses accordingly so that my costs didn't increase as my revenue increased.

Since 2019, I've made bigger financial gains by being very intentional with how money is reinvested in the business. Instead of throwing money at things I want to happen, I pay myself a professional salary, prioritize paying my team well, and save money for the future.

While my own business intentions were not to stay solo, my experience is all too common for owners of solo businesses too. I share this story as I see it all the time.

THE IMPACT OF EXPENSE CREEP

We don't talk nearly enough about the impact of expense creep on our bottom line and our feelings about our business and day-to-day life.

When you're paying everyone else but not bringing home enough money on an ongoing basis, it's a one-way ticket to resentment and business burnout.

Much of entrepreneurship is rooted in the idea that you must constantly "invest" in your business, and it's normalized to spend money on tools, programs, and coaches when you'd be better served paying yourself.

That may seem overly simplistic, but there's far too much emphasis on the capitalist mantra "you need to spend money to make money." That message gets tied up with our desire to live a comfortable, joyful life, then baits us into consistently spending money to chase that dream.

The irony is that, in many cases, the dream is within reach if we would only stop and recognize that we're funding other people's lives while often getting very little in return.

I asked Certified Public Accountant (CPA) Erin Rue the biggest money struggles she sees with solo business owners, and she said the income statement is generally where energy is focused:

"What happens is they think that their net income is what should be in their bank account, but what they aren't understanding is how cash flows through their business. So when they go to take money out for themselves (or pay taxes) the cash they were expecting isn't actually available."

This is why salary is a cornerstone of staying solo, as for you to thrive, you need to pay yourself a consistent, reliable salary first.

You simply can't have a sustainable solo business if you're not getting paid for your work.

SET SALARY GOALS BEFORE REVENUE GOALS

For every kind of business, it's common to set an annual or monthly revenue goal. This is a way to establish a clear plan for how much money you want to make.

However, revenue goals are often set either arbitrarily or aspirationally. We can easily find ourselves chasing a revenue number without it having real meaning, or worse yet, sacrificing our salary to reach that goal.

We've all heard stories about founders not drawing a salary or putting all their money back into the business. This narrative is common in entrepreneurship, but it's a highly unrealistic one for the majority of solo, lifestyle-driven entrepreneurs.

Most people don't have the runway to not draw a salary from the business for very long. That kind of space is a luxury. Consultant Sharon Zimmerman found herself sacrificing her pay: "It made it a struggle to even participate in my personal life. Being able to pay myself from my business is a core priority. Even if it's a small amount that week or that month, I do it anyway."

While there is some level of risk in the early stages of starting a business, I don't believe that anyone should be chasing revenue metrics over paying themselves.

Before setting a revenue goal, I recommend you determine a personal salary goal. This approach has you setting your budget for expenses and your revenue goals based on the draw you need to be taking from the business on a monthly basis.

As accountant and interim CFO Connie Vanderzanden shared with me, "The business needs to contribute to your life. When we avoid paying ourselves we are not living up to the agreement we have with our business. So while reinvesting back into our business for growth seems like the best course of action — we'll just go 30 days, 90 days, 6 months, 1 year without being paid because that's normal — it's not sustainable. Eventually if your business is not contributing to your life it will result in resentment; you won't show up which in turn means the business will suffer, maybe even force you to go back and get a job."

Setting Your Salary Goal

You didn't start a business to *not* get paid. Or for you to pay an overpriced coach or for your clients to get a subsidized rate while you can't pay the rent this month.

My goal is to help you pay yourself a professional salary and base your revenue goal on that first and foremost.

You should consider your ideal "enough" number to determine your salary goal.

As part of this exercise, I want you to consider how you can avoid being trapped in a cycle of conspicuous consumption, acquiring goods and services far beyond your needs. I fully understand this can be challenging thanks to the fact that we're conditioned to "keep up with the Joneses."

The phrase which appeared in a 1913 comic strip is more true today than ever. Where once we could only see what those in our immediate community were buying, with social media we have a glimpse into others' lives, including those of celebrities, around the world.

While you may not be enticed to buy the latest product a Kardashian is promoting, you likely look to your peers for cues on what you should be doing with your life and business. Social comparison theory is the idea that "individuals determine their own social and personal worth based on how they stack up against others."

It's a tricky balancing act as while we don't want to fall into this trap, we need to find our "enough" where, in the words of anti-capitalist business coach Bear Hebert, we're "balancing justice and liberation with being financially secure."

Before we get into the math, please know I'm not going to tell you what that number should be. It will vary dramatically based on your unique situation. Still, I want to remind you that so many of the revenue goals in online business — looking at you, six figures! — are arbitrary.

In the Staying Solo Starter Kit accompanying this book, you'll find a calculator designed to help you crunch the numbers to determine your desired salary goal. If anything isn't applicable, you can input a zero. (Grab your copy of the kit at www.stayingsolokit.com)

When using this web-based tool, if you're unsure what number to use for your taxes, I recommend you consult an accountant or bookkeeper to provide guidance. Most tax agencies have easy-to-find tax tables that outline your tax rate.

By working with the numbers, you can identify the best way to achieve your personal salary goal based on your specific situation and not the magical thinking prevalent in online business.

And if you're unclear on your numbers, it's time to make that a priority. As Connie Vanderzanden says, "It becomes harder to find a stable footing when you don't know what the real numbers are. Taking time to put something in writing that you can use to measure actual against, will go a long way to answering questions like: Can I afford this? Do I have enough to pay myself? What do I pay myself? Not having the numbers may result in financial anxiety, which the majority of us have. Getting support for this initial plan and brainstorming about what will be created will be really beneficial for that long-term sustainability factor."

HOW MUCH SHOULD I PAY MYSELF?

Determining how much to pay yourself is complex. I can't tackle that question with a blanket answer. However, I can remind you that you're a professional service provider and should be paid as such.

CPA Erin Rue recommends starting with "what you know you need to bring in to cover your living expenses and financial goals (debt paydown, savings) and then factor in a bump up amount for cushion. This means getting *very* clear about what your real household expenses are. The tracking doesn't have to be complex or overly difficult. Start with something like YNAB (a tool for budgeting) and just do the basics and get more detailed as you get comfortable with the process. It works for business cash flow planning as well in a simplified manner."

The exact number will vary based on your industry, role, experience, current business situation, and personal factors such as where you live. You should base the number on your specific needs, and remember, it's safe for you to be paid like a professional.

So many service business owners I encounter have solid revenue in their business but continue to underpay themselves. They will keep cash in the company beyond what they could realistically need, which they could be paying themselves.

Remember, 86.3% of small business owners said they take a yearly salary of less than $100,000.

In the past, I've had clients look at what they would be paid for their corporate role, which has been an eye-opener. They can see how they're not being greedy but rather that they should be paying themselves more.

If you wish you could pay yourself more, but your revenue won't support it, let this encourage you to see that it's possible. Avoid comparing yourself to others, and know you may need some tweaks to achieve that desired salary goal.

Why You May Not Be Paying Yourself

Before we get into the nuts and bolts of talking about paying yourself, I want to address why many solo business owners aren't paying themselves consistently. It would be irresponsible for me not to address these reasons as part of this discussion.

Sometimes, it's a lack of clients that prevents you from paying yourself. In this case, there needs to be a proactive marketing plan put in place to get you in front of your target audience. I don't want to belabor the point, but the reality is that you can't sit and wait for clients to come to you. You need to be proactive about how you find clients.

If you're proactively doing marketing and feel you don't have the potential clients you need, consider whether your messaging, website, or offers are clear and compelling.

Also, dig into each of your marketing activities to assess if it's the right fit. For example, if you're getting inquiries from Instagram but they are all the wrong fit for your services, that may not be the right channel for you, and it could be time to switch things up.

While marketing takes time, it is unsustainable to continue activities that aren't producing potential client leads. The 80/20 rule applies to your marketing efforts, meaning 80% of your outcomes will come from 20% of your activities. Figure out what 20% is driving results and go further. Adding more and more marketing is a recipe for wasted time and energy.

Another reason you may not be able to pay yourself comes down to your pricing. If you have a full client roster and need to make more money, something has to give. That's unsustainable too and only ramps up the resentment.

When I talk to service providers who want to burn down their business, it's because they have a full client roster and still aren't making enough money.

The global economy is a rollercoaster, which sometimes impacts business spending decisions. However, that doesn't mean you can't adjust your pricing, especially with new clients coming in the door.

Don't make the mistake of deciding no one will pay your new rate, as there will always be clients willing to pay that rate — within reason of course!

If you're unsure about pricing, I recommend you use the salary goal we're discussing to help you clearly see how you need to price your services.

As one of my mentors said, "We're running a business, not a non-profit. You need to price things so we get paid appropriately."

The Psychology of Money

A final reason you may not be paying yourself is your money stories, or even financial trauma. This isn't about the flippant money mindset and manifestation advice that's all over Instagram and TikTok, but rather the very real conditions that impact how we think and feel about money.

Each one of us has stories and scripts related to our money. In some cases, we may have experienced traumatic events around money. Chantel Chapman, the co-founder and CEO of Trauma of Money, defines financial trauma as "an emotional wounding that happens as a direct result of something to do specifically with money."

In my experience, money-related issues impact entrepreneurs so deeply that I invested in Chapman's Trauma of Money program to become a professional facilitator. Money trauma may be the result of poverty, divorce, abuse, sudden changes in financial situations, and other factors.

Other times, we've learned and internalized our money stories throughout our life.

A great example is one of the biggest motivations for my becoming an entrepreneur. I grew up lower middle class, and while the basics were covered, there weren't many extras. There were times of major financial instability in our family, particularly throughout my teens and early twenties.

I'll spare you all the details, but this resulted in knowing from a relatively young age that I didn't want to ever depend on anyone else for money. Decades later, I carry that with me as I have little patience for anyone that screws with my money. The experience I have had around money trauma means it's very easy for me to default into a cycle of overwork as I associate having more money with being secure.

THE MECHANICS OF PAYING YOURSELF

As always, I want to remind you that I'm not a money, tax, or accounting professional; this tool is to be used as a starting point. I've been running my own business for over 18 years, and I've been able to pay myself a healthy salary every single year.

I want you to be able to do the same by setting goals around your money, expenses, and salary that put you first.

While I'm not a finance or accounting professional, there are some basics that I've had to learn as a business owner, so here's a run down on the most common questions solo business owners have about paying themselves.

#1. How and When Should I Pay Myself?

With that in mind, I often get asked how and when entrepreneurs should pay themselves. The mechanics of this will largely depend on how your business is set up. You may need to put yourself on payroll or be in a situation where you can draw from your business accounts.

Whether it's payroll or draws, please set a frequency on which you pay yourself, such as twice a month or biweekly. If you're not doing that consistently, you may need to build up some cash in the business to start doing that.

I want to remind you that dealing with money can be loaded, so it's entirely normal if you're having the feels about this. If need be, start small so you can consistently pay yourself, and then you can increase the amount over time as you feel more comfortable.

Trust me when I say this. When you're paying yourself on a set schedule, you'll feel more secure in your business as you see the results of your work in your personal bank account.

If you're not separating your business and personal money, do that as soon as possible so you start to see the business money as its own bucket.

To quote bookkeeper Misa Bacon from Perfectly Kept Books, "Never spend money directly out of the business for personal expenses. Always make sure money moves from the business account to a personal account. This keeps business and personal separate."

#2. Should I Use Personal Money to Pay For Things?

When you're starting your business, you'll need some startup funds from your personal bank account. Ideally, that should be a one-time event and treated as a "loan" that gets repaid.

I strongly recommend that you curb the urge to cash flow anything in your business with personal funds. It's a slippery slope as we often don't have access to capital in our business at first, but we have access to debt in our personal lives.

My rule has always been that the business needs to pay for its own expenses. There may be minor exceptions along the way, but using personal funds for the business can quickly create more significant issues beyond being unable to pay yourself.

#3. What's a Good Profit Margin?

For your profit margin, there is no blanket answer. I encourage you to consult with a qualified professional to discuss the specifics of your situation.

What I can tell you is that as a solopreneur, your expenses should not be eating up the majority of your revenue. In the simplest terms, your profit margin matters as it's what will enable you to pay yourself.

When I asked Misa Bacon about this, she provided insights on the topic: "There are various considerations that go into how 'good' of a profit margin a business will have, but a good rule of thumb is 20% or more would be considered a healthy profit margin. Service businesses in particular typically have higher profit margins than other businesses due to the nature of the business and fewer costs overall."

Remember, to be able to accurately calculate your profit margin you need the right data in place. Erin Rue recommends that you have "a solid accounting structure in place that's updated regularly and is accurate," as she often sees business owners not paying attention to their books. This results in "making decisions from inaccurate amounts, paying more in taxes or not being able to pay themselves."

#4. How Much Should I Budget for Expenses?

Your business expenses directly impact your ability to pay yourself, so my advice is for you to carefully consider each and every expense. When doing your budget, I would reverse engineer your expenses by deciding what you need to pay yourself first, and then dividing your expenses into two categories: necessities and nice-to-haves.

Necessities are the items you require to do your work. For example, if you're a designer, this may be your licence for Adobe's Creative Cloud Suite. Your necessities are what you absolutely can't live without on an ongoing basis.

The nice-to-haves are the tools, support, and other expenses that make your life easier. You *can* do your day-to-day work without them, but they boost your productivity, save you time, and so on. These are the types of budget items I recommend my clients tie to their revenue; which ones you have depend on what your revenue looks like year-over-year.

For example, let's say you want to work with a specific coach but it's going to stretch your budget, and if you say yes right now it will require you to pay yourself less, and you're not prepared to swing it. Instead of investing and hoping the revenue needed to pay for that expense will follow, I would wait until a time when you can comfortably make that investment.

#5. What About Taxes?

My clients love to ask me about taxes, and this is one area where I'm not prepared to tell you what to do. How much you set aside for taxes will depend on what type of business entity you have, along with where you live, so this is well worth a paid consultation with an accounting professional.

With that in mind, I do recommend your tax liabilities are considered when it comes to both your budgeting and your pricing. As the saying goes, "nothing is certain but death and taxes," so you need to plan accordingly.

Misa Bacon recommends that you maintain your bookkeeping monthly so you have a clear picture of what's going on with the business, and that you have a trusted tax professional to advise on how to best handle it.

Getting professional tax advice, along with bookkeeping, was the first investment I made in my business, and it's worth every penny to have peace of mind.

"Don't be afraid to work with professionals just because it's going to cost money. I see so many people who DIY their entity setup, taxes, accounting, and other areas and then get themselves into trouble. It ends up costing more money to undo mistakes than it would have cost just to have a consultation at the beginning and do it right from the start," Erin Rue explains.

"There are free and low-cost options for business owners to get help (like at SCORE or Small Business Development Centers in the US) so there's really no excuse to not get the help and advice needed to get set up correctly. Please stop taking TikTok advice from a 60-second video where someone is dancing and pointing."

LET'S GET YOU PAID

There's a reason why I'm talking about salary as the first pillar of the Staying Solo® Framework. If you're not getting paid appropriately, it's hard to make solid business decisions. It's challenging to show up every day and serve your clients.

While you may not be at your desired salary goal today, you have the power to make decisions quickly and take action. That may be reducing your expenses, doing more marketing to bring in more clients, fixing your pricing, or simply paying yourself in a more structured way.

"Be proactive and pay attention to what's happening financially from the beginning because the numbers will always tell you the true story of what's going on in your business and how to make better decisions," shared Misa Bacon. "It's okay to ask for help when you have questions or don't understand something. Having your bookkeeping on point and the right financial team in your corner will allow you to thrive in business and pay your desired salary."

By working the numbers, you can plan for what needs to happen so you are getting paid and your needs are being met. No one starts a business not to make money, and I want to give you the know-how you need to create a solo business that's sustainable for years to come.

Chapter 5

Carving Out Consistent Space

S ervice business owners often think that the "service" part of the business model means they have to run themselves ragged serving their clients. Or that they need to work around the clock to reach their goals. Nothing could be further from the truth.

Space. There's nothing quite like that feeling of having space. Of knowing you have the time, energy, and even physical environment you need on a day-to-day basis.

When you run a business, it's easy to constantly fill up your space. To cram your calendar full of busywork, to say yes when you should say no, to compromise your emotional and energetic needs and so on.

Unsurprisingly, this happens when so much of the narrative around entrepreneurship is about hustling to make things happen. Think of the stories of the "great" entrepreneurs we hear about constantly. They focus on long hours and the constant sacrifices required to make the dream a reality, but on the flip side there's this message about freedom and 4-hour work weeks.

> The plot twist is that these stories are essentially fairy tales. Entrepreneurship comes at a grave cost to many people.

THE RISKY REALITY OF ENTREPRENEURSHIP

A 2015 study by Freeman and others examined the prevalence of mental health issues amongst entrepreneurs, with 72% of participants self-reporting mental health issues including depression and substance abuse.

More recently, the 2021 FLIK Mental Health of Female Founders Report found that women and non-binary participants reported a lack of work/life balance and a "lifestyle of burnout and anxiety." 52% of respondents reported dealing with mental health issues including depression (36.6%) and anxiety (33.3%).

It's worth noting that there is a bit of a chicken or egg situation here, as many of us with mental health challenges are drawn to entrepreneurship or find that self-employment is really our best possible option.

Shulamit Ber Levtov, a therapist specializing in entrepreneurship and mental health, shares that "mental health challenges are a risk inherent in entrepreneurship."

From my point of view, conventional teachings about how entrepreneurship "should be" only add to that risk and negatively impact our mental health.

As business owners, we need to pre-empt this risk and ensure that we're making and not falling into the trap of the "shoulds." We need to carve out space to do things our way and not compromise our mental health in the process.

The Horrors of Hustle Culture

Confession: For years I prided myself on being a hustler and on my work ethic. I liked being known as someone who would work hard to make things happen.

Welcome to hustle culture. Where we measure our worth in hours worked and tasks completed, and our lives revolve around our to-do list.

While hustle culture may be the natural consequence of late stage capitalism, there's been a greater awareness in recent years that this endless hustle leads to extreme stress, anxiety, and burnout.

I'm still untangling my worth from my productivity, and as Brittany Berger writes in a blog post on divesting from hustle culture, "internalized capitalism, workaholism, and productivity dysphoria isn't something you can 'just shake off' in a weekend or two."

Hustle culture is toxic and always makes us feel like whatever work we're doing is never enough.

As nutritionist Sarah Berneche expands, "It makes me feel like what I'm doing isn't enough — I don't have enough followers, I don't produce enough content, I don't have enough income streams and so on."

As a business owner, you have an opportunity to unlearn hustle culture and do things differently. And that starts with proactively managing your space.

SPACE IS ABOUT CREATING CAPACITY

For solo business owners, space is a necessary, non-negotiable piece of the puzzle, and this is why I have included it in the Staying Solo® Framework.

When you hear the word "space," you likely think of your calendar or not having every minute of your day booked — which is just the start.

The traditional approach to capacity within a business is about balancing the supply and demand of your time and the work you've committed to doing. For service business owners, this is typically a balancing act of ensuring you're booked out, but not overbooked to the point that you need to work constantly.

For example, if you want to work 20 hours a week, that's your "supply" of hours. Then for demand, you have four clients, all needing a minimum of 5 hours per week. In this scenario, you're over capacity, because you have not accounted for the time you need to actually run your business.

The supply vs. demand equation for capacity is fundamentally imperfect as client demands can fluctuate week by week, as will your supply of available hours.

In reality, inputs such as available hours, time required, and schedules only get you so far. While they can't be ignored, they only share part of the equation. If we only focus on this part of things — particularly as solo business owners — we're likely to feel like we never have space.

Becca Rich, a holistic time management coach, says that business owners have an adversarial relationship with their calendar. As she puts it, business owners "get into a cycle where they create an extremely optimistic schedule, fill it to the brim with work and shoulds, and expect to follow it perfectly. Then when life inevitably comes up and time blocks need to move, many feel guilty about it. Most if not all parts of this cycle are influenced by narratives steeped in hustle-and-grind culture. Our calendars reflect an internalized desire to fit 'everything' in and be hyper-productive."

In recent years, I've come to recognize that many of my clients don't have an issue with time; they have an ongoing challenge with capacity. We need to stop looking at capacity as an equation that we can solve and lean into finding ways to create and manage more space within our businesses and lives. As long as we treat time as the enemy, we're going to struggle.

How we've been taught to approach time is fundamentally broken, and it leaves us struggling and feeling like we're never ever going to get it all done.

As Becca Rich explains, "Traditional time management advice focuses on generic, one-size-fits-all strategies that don't consider an individual's work styles, priorities, and circumstances. Most of the time, it also overlooks the importance of factors like energy levels, motivation, and personal values."

In the context of staying solo, space is about creating capacity for you to:

- Step away from the business including daily, weekly, and throughout the year.
- Free up your calendar so there's freedom to work on the business, including creative and strategy work you'd like to be doing.
- Manage your capacity beyond your time, including your energy and emotions.

These three pillars may seem unattainable to you right now, but they're essential to being able to build a sustainable service business.

Without space, you're stuck in a cycle of constant hustle, frustration, overwhelm, or worse yet, burnout.

I'm not going to deny that very real systemic factors may impact your ability to create this capacity in the short term, but starting to take even baby steps to reclaim space in your business and life can go a long way.

Now, let's dig a bit more into each of these elements.

Stepping Away From the Business

Running a business can be all-consuming for many of us. Sometimes that's simply a matter of survival; other times, it's because we've bought into the idea that we need to make ever-increasing sums of money to succeed.

A 2023 report from the Canadian Federation of Independent Business found that small business owners work the equivalent of an eight-day work week, or 54 hours per week.

A survey from cloud-based accounting software provider Xero reported that small business owners were more likely than the average American worker to stay connected while on vacation, with only 14% completely disconnecting. The same study found that 55% of business owners take two weeks or less of vacation per year.

Whatever the underlying motivation for being unwilling to step away from the business, I want you to know that you *need* to do this. Long hours, no days off, and never being disconnected aren't just unhealthy — they're counterproductive.

This comes down to the law of diminishing returns where investing more time or energy into your business results in a proportionally smaller return.

So if you work 60 hours a week instead of 30 hours, you're likely not moving the needle the way you think you are. The quality of your work and your clients' experiences are likely to suffer.

A 2014 study from John Penavel indicates that long hours don't yield greater output and productivity freefalls beyond 50 hours a week.

Furthermore, multiple studies link overwork to a host of physical and mental health issues. The harsh truth is that even if you're not dealing with acute health conditions, you're putting yourself at higher risk of getting run down, sick, or burnt out.

Plus, when we're overworking, we're doing things that make us feel like we're making progress when we're really wasting time on things that don't matter. The 80/20 rule applies here too, with 20% of your activities driving 80% of your results.

So please, go take some time away already!

With that out of the way, you're likely wondering what specifically I mean by "time away." If we look at this from a calendar perspective, as that's a unit of measurement we all understand, you should have time "off" from the business.

DAILY: You need downtime every day. Working all day every day is not sustainable. Your body and brain will suffer if you do this. If you have "free time," find a hobby and resist the urge to work just because you can. Set hours of work and stick to them as much as possible.

WEEKLY: Every single week you should have set days off. Again, you need time to rest, reset, and have a life. If you want to work on the weekend (or that's better for your schedule), compensate for it during the week. Studies about the four-day workweek consistently reveal how it reduces stress, illness, and burnout.

YEARLY: We all need regular time away from the business that's more than a weekend. So many solo business owners fall into the trap of thinking they can't take time away as clients "need" them, but it's completely untrue. If you had a traditional job, you'd take a vacation, and your clients should expect you to do the same. Period. Clients who are not okay with this are not clients you need to have.

You're likely reading this with a bit of skepticism and thinking this is something you can do later, but as holistic time coach Becca Rich reminds us, "One-day thinking causes us to push off rest, relaxation, and enjoyment until after 'everything gets done.' Thus the hustle and grind hamster wheel is created. We're left feeling not good enough. And forever short on time."

Remember, you don't need to earn your rest or time away from work. Period.

While this message is slowly coming into the mainstream, I want to acknowledge that it's only thanks to the hard work of Black and disabled individuals bringing forth this conversation as a matter of their survival.

Creating space in this way is not about just being able to work harder or faster, but having a vibrant life. You're more than your work or business.

Free Up Your Calendar

A common trap that most service business owners fall into is trying to fill their time with client work. I get it. I did this in a big way in the early years of my business as I wanted to maximize my "billable" time.

I failed to understand that I needed time to do more than client work and that working for clients all day for most of the week was holding me back in many ways. At first, I didn't do very much to work "on" the business. My best work was being done for my clients, and my business got the leftovers.

Building a sustainable business requires us to do more than simply deliver for clients. We need to focus on the marketing, sales, and service aspects of our business so we can find clients, refine our systems, sell more efficiently, develop new offers, and more.

In an assessment I use with my solopreneur clients, I ask them how much time they spend on non-client work in an average week. Here is what they said:

- 26% one hour or less
- 21% two to three hours
- 37% three to five hours
- 16% over five hours

What this reveals is how little time, on average, they spend on the actual business. To put this in context, if you work 30 hours a week and spend three hours working on your business, that's only 10% of your time.

When I worked in an agency environment, I was expected as an entry level employee to bill 80% of my time and had a 20% margin for other tasks. As a business owner, you have way more to do than I ever did as an account coordinator, so you need to give yourself room to actually do it.

Your business deserves more than the dregs of your day. This is why you must commit time every month (ideally each week) to work on the business. Personally, I reserve different time blocks during the week for marketing/creative work, strategic work, and research or even thinking time.

Many of my clients use theme days or set aside a week a month to focus on the business. You may need to experiment with approaches that work best for you and your brain, so keep an open mind until you find something that sticks.

As Becca Rich shared with me, "Remember, time management simply comes down to clarifying how you truly want to spend your time, finding the right strategies and tools that support you, and then doing it compassionately and imperfectly."

How to Work On Your Business

If this is new to you, you can start by setting aside some time for whatever element of the business needs your attention now and go from there. I highly recommend you protect that time at all costs. You're not available for meetings, client questions, or anything else. No one needs to know what you're doing; you're simply unavailable during that time.

At first, or if you're trying again to implement this, it's not uncommon to feel like you can't free up this time as you need to be billing. That's a sign that you may need to examine your pricing structure, as no business should base their rates on filling every hour.

You need to price your services to enable you to have the space on your calendar to run the business. If you have 30 available hours to work per week on average, you should not be booking 30 hours worth of client work. At a minimum, you should be reserving 25% of your available time for running the business.

If the idea of reserving that 25% of your time seems completely unrealistic for you right now, start smaller. Even a 5% improvement in your capacity to work on the business is a win.

As a business owner, this is where your boundaries are critical. It's very easy to let your clients dictate how and when you work, but you need to remember this is your business, and you get to set the pace. (More on boundaries coming up in Chapter 13.)

Managing Your Capacity Beyond Time

As we've discussed, space as a concept for those who want to stay solo is about more than time. When you're working to create capacity, your energy, emotions, and sensory needs should be considered.

I tend to default to looking at capacity as being about time as it's a neat and tidy unit of measurement. But I find myself struggling when I rely too heavily on it and don't account for my energetic or emotional capacity. I will set out the plan for the "perfect" week with very little wiggle room for less-than-optimal conditions.

Guess what — that's a recipe for disaster, frustration, annoyance, and a host of other emotions when the plan doesn't go exactly as I want.

This is why you need to be radically realistic about how your energy, emotions, and sensory needs impact your work and plan accordingly. This is exceptionally important for those who live with a disability, are neurodivergent, or are managing their mental health.

Brittany Berger, a mental health advocate and the founder of Work Brighter (which works with neurodivergent, chronically ill, and disabled professionals to help balance productivity, rest, and self-care), says, "You really have to understand your body and brain's limits. So much of it depends on your ability. There's so much our bodies and brains are doing on a daily basis other than working that we don't even realize during our day-to-day lives how much time is spent. We need to stop moralizing productivity as it doesn't have any real moral value."

Berger shares that it wasn't possible for her to grow a business with the mindset of work being the "way to worthiness" and just doing increasingly more to chase a goal. "I've felt like a lot of people didn't understand my limits. People minimizing and bypassing the realities of my disability and not listening to what I say about my capacity has been a challenge. It often gets written off as mindset blocks."

Prioritizing Your Needs as a Human

Many of my clients start their business as a way to ensure they're able to care for themselves as humans who are disabled and/or neurodivergent. Yet, as Brittany Berger says, so much of the standard business advice is "like fast fashion but for professional development."

From the insufficient scope of self-care to hot takes on how to schedule your day as an ADHDer, that advice didn't work for Brittany, and it won't work for many like her.

Case in point: I know it doesn't work for me. I'm by no means an expert on this topic beyond my lived experience with anxiety, depression, and ADHD, as well as physical and learning disabilities. All of these impact my work, as well as my capacity on a daily basis.

While more and more of us recognize that the hustle culture approach to running a business is unsustainable, it can be a struggle to find alternative approaches that honour our abilities and capacity.

I asked ADHD coach Amelie Leveille about some of the common challenges faced by solo business owners with ADHD: "We struggle with building routines around repetitive tasks such as money or time management. Being solo makes this particularly hard because we have to build our own framework and routines, as no one is there to keep us on track."

One of my least favourite tropes is that, as an entrepreneur, you need to get up at 5 am to rise and grind. When you consider that someone with ADHD struggles with routine, this type of advice isn't just unhelpful, but likely inaccessible and sets us up for failure.

Does that mean you can't build a routine if you have ADHD? Absolutely not, but you need to recognize what comes easily to you, and where you may struggle.

As Leveille says, "Entrepreneurs with ADHD are usually creative and great problem solvers. They need to watch for self-criticism that stops them from doing what they're good at."

Zoe Linda is a great example of a solo business owner who's actively worked to recognize the space she needs business-wise, blending services and products to help manage her capacity. As someone who lives with a disability, she's very careful about ensuring whatever she sells will work for her:

"When offering day rates for eight hours, they were frequently rolling over to the next day. I wasn't doing my best work as halfway through the day I'd be watching the clock. I was so tired and counting down the hours. I decided to spread the eight hours over two days for the same price and it's been great."

The reality is that there are many factors that impact your capacity, and you need to do what works best for you. There are no gold stars for pushing beyond your capacity, and absolutely no benefit to adhering to bullshit ideas of how you should be doing things in your business, or as a human.

DIFFERENT TYPES OF CAPACITY TO CONSIDER

The majority of the time when people talk to me about being "over" their capacity, they're referring to being overbooked and overwhelmed.

The way we're conditioned, we tend to go back to a lack of time as a reason that this happens, but it's about so much more than our time. Our energetic, emotional, and sensory capacity are just as important as our time. They all work together to support us as multi-faceted, complex beings.

Not all of the below types of capacity may be applicable to everyone, but tuning into which ones are impacting your ability to create space for yourself within your business can make a major difference.

Energetic Capacity	Emotional Capacity	Sensory Capacity
• Work schedule and hours • The intensity of the work you do • Need for rest/recovery • Daily ups/downs • Seasonal cycles • Physical ability or disability • Ability to concentrate/be attentive	• Types of work you do • Types of clients • Receiving feedback • Being seen/visible • Life stress • Living up to your personal expectations	• Your workspace • Level of peopling • Comms systems • Technology • Processing information • Level of repetition • Ability to create systems

Energetic Capacity

If there's a lesson I've had to learn as a business owner, it's that my energetic capacity varies dramatically by day, week, and season. While that is influenced by the fact I'm a neurodivergent introvert, we all have different energetic capacities and it's determined by a number of factors.

Your energetic capacity is defined as the energy required to get your work done. This is why factors such as your work schedule and the type of work you do impact how much you can accomplish on any given day.

This isn't about finding a way to be more productive, but rather recognizing that you're human. You need to set up the conditions that you need to thrive.

Brittany Berger says one of the first steps to dismantling our toxic relationship with productivity is our energy management: "I'm an autistic introvert. One hour of Zoom calls for me, that's the equivalent of like eight hours spent writing. Why would I do that to myself?"

Using the example of calls, if you find you can only handle two calls in a day because they drain you, scheduling four calls in a day is going to suck the life out of you. Or if you know you work best when you stick to a four-day work week, but you keep adding "one more thing" that results in a fifth or six day of work, you're missing out on opportunities to rest.

No one trick that works when it comes to managing your energy, as your needs shift based on the seasons, your mental and physical health, hormonal cycles, and countless other factors. To expect you're going to show up every single day, with the same amount of energy, and do the exact same amount of work is completely unrealistic.

Yet, that's the pressure we put on ourselves as solo business owners. In thinking about your energetic capacity, consider how you can prioritize based on how much energy you need at any given time. Sometimes I've found the most "productive" thing I can do is to choose to not work and instead take a nap.

Remember, as a business owner, you have a degree of flexibility that other people don't have. You're not automatically required to work 9 to 5, Monday to Friday like with traditional employment. You can adapt to manage your energy in a way that best serves you and your clients.

Entrepreneurship and energy isn't one-size-fits-all, yet so many times we're pushed towards these rigid schedules that don't work for us. A great example of this is the idea that to be our most productive and successful selves, we need to get up at 5 am and execute a list of high performance tasks.

No shade to the early birds reading this book, but I'm not someone who's able to maintain that type of schedule for any length of time. As someone who does creative work, trying to do that work first thing in the morning doesn't work for me, and frankly, it's a waste of time as I'm not creative until midday. I do some of my best writing in the evenings no matter how much I try to do it earlier.

It's a matter of energetic capacity and figuring out what works for you. If you're more of a night owl, why are you trying to do your best work at 5 am and making yourself miserable?

In considering your energetic capacity, ask these questions:

- What's boosting my energy? What's draining it?
- How's my energy level right now? How has it been this month or week?
- Is my schedule aligned with my energetic rhythm?
- Am I doing enough to recharge my energy?
- Are my expectations for my level of energy realistic?
- What else can I be doing to protect my energy?

Emotional Capacity

Working hand-in-hand with your energetic capacity is your emotional capacity, your ability to "experience a wide range of emotions and handle difficult feelings without falling apart."

Alison Brabban, a consulting clinical psychologist, and Dr. Douglas Turkington, a consulting psychiatrist, created the concept of the Stress and Vulnerability Bucket to identify and treat relapses of mental illness. The idea is that the fuller our bucket is, the less able we are to deal with stress, and we need a healthy way to allow stress to flow out of the bucket.

As a business owner, you're subject to many stressors on an ongoing basis, and we can all tolerate different levels of stress. Which is why we need to be cognizant of our unique level of emotional capacity at any given time.

Essentially, you want to be able to set your work up in a way that helps minimize needless stress and doesn't stretch your emotional capacity too far.

For any service business owner, this may mean finding ways to do work that you enjoy or fuels you creatively, or maintaining boundaries so that you limit stressful situations.

For example, if you're a writer and you can only work on one big project at a time, but you keep booking three that go on simultaneously, you need to find ways to better manage how and when you work.

It's worth noting that sometimes you may discover that the actual type of work you've chosen to do is misaligned with your emotional capacity. This isn't uncommon where people are in "helping" roles that are emotionally taxing and which they can't sustain over time.

Another common challenge faced by business owners is a pattern of working with clients that are emotionally challenging. Sometimes this will be more subtle as you have a client who complains excessively, wastes your time, or insists on micromanaging you. Other times, it can be much more confronting as they violate boundaries or are downright disrespectful.

At any given time, your threshold for dealing with emotionally draining clients will vary, but I want to remind you that there is no situation in which you need to tolerate client behavior that's causing you stress, or making you feel unsafe.

As someone with ADHD, I experience a phenomenon called rejection sensitive dysphoria, where I experience emotional pain when I feel rejected. My brain is dysregulated and can take things like feedback or perceived criticisms personally.

With clients, I've had to put a structured process in place for feedback on any written work so it's managed in a way that works for me. This has the added benefit of ensuring that I'm receiving the feedback in a written versus verbal format, as I find it extremely challenging to process edits to my work without seeing them.

When thinking about your emotional capacity, consider how you can interact with and receive feedback from clients that doesn't cause stress and aligns with your learning style and the way you best process information. Otherwise you may find you're experiencing stress, or even an emotional response.

Finally, owning a business means that you need to "put yourself out there," but what happens when your emotional capacity to do so is limited? The majority of business advice assumes that we're all able to "show up" the same way without recognizing the toll it can take.

The focus is always on the positive impacts of visibility such as building trust and brand recognition, but not on the potential downsides of public scrutiny, loss of privacy, increased pressure, and even potentially burnout.

I've personally experienced the downside of being visible as I market my business, with critique of my voice and appearance, as well as people actively fighting with me online. What I've dealt with is minor compared to what some people face, and I have the emotional capacity to deal with it in a healthy way.

When considering how you market or share your business, you want to find an approach that addresses your emotional capacity while ensuring you're not causing needless stress, or even being unsafe.

Mai-kee Tsang created the concept of Sustainable Visibility® after recognizing that the ways entrepreneurs are taught to be visible online are falling short. As she explains, "What people don't realize is that every visibility opportunity can be a liability. They don't think about the aftermath of how much capacity it is going to take to honor what may come because we want to be visible. We need to put safety first, strategy second."

Questions to consider:

- What triggers my stress?
- How am I feeling right now?
- Is this realistic for me?
- Am I setting boundaries with my clients?
- Am I in an emotional state where it's safe to be seen?

Sensory Capacity

A couple of years ago, I was hosting an in-person retreat with several members of one of my masterminds. The conversation turned to how people were managing different sensory issues, with so many practical ideas being shared from what ear plugs people liked to office lighting.

This is a prime example of how real sensory inputs impact us as humans, as well as impacting the work we do. As with everything, this varies for each of us, but if you're someone who gets overstimulated due to noise or too many calls in a day, it's time to be more proactive about managing your sensory capacity.

One of the best parts of being the boss is that for the most part you control the environment you work in, so you have the power to set yourself up for success. Consider what may cause distraction or discomfort for you, such as lighting, noise, temperature, or specific stimuli. All of these can, and should, be managed over time.

Ask yourself the following questions to explore your sensory capacity:

- What may be causing me to be distracted or stressed?
- Is there anything I can adjust in my workspace to be more comfortable?
- What's out of my control but I can take measures to manage?
- How can I build in rest or take breaks to change sensory inputs?
- Am I taking care of my physical needs such as eating, drinking, and rest so my sensory well-being is cared for?

THERE'S NO SUSTAINABILITY WITHOUT SPACE

The traditional approach to time management or productivity is rooted in focusing on doing more, when sustainability as a service business owner relies on you freeing up space to do things aside from client work.

If you're deeply entrenched in the world of productivity hacks and time management tips, this may require a shift towards thinking less about your time and more about how you can use that time to create space to work on the business, to be away from the business, and generally work in a way that serves you better.

When you're able to focus on running your business as a solopreneur in a way that gives you space, you'll do better work for your clients, you'll be more creative, you'll enjoy what you've built, and most of all, you'll ensure that you're protecting your most valuable asset, you.

Chapter 6

Rethinking Planning to Focus on Seasons

Most of us start our businesses for more flexibility and freedom, but somewhere along the way, we find that we're trapped in a cycle of hustling. To stay solo, you need a realistic planning process that works for you and keeps you from chasing things that simply don't matter to you.

I've talked about planning as long as I've had a blog or podcast. And the truth is that I have a love/hate relationship with it. Sometimes we're hot and heavy, and other times I want to completely ignore it.

In my early days as a solo business owner, I'll be honest, I didn't really see the point. I felt I could only plan so much as a team of one. While I'd plan my personal life carefully (yes, I'm a little type A), I felt like my professional life was somewhat at the whims of my clients.

When I landed in the online business world, I found myself among people who loved to plan their businesses. They planned like it was an Olympic sport and that started to rub off on me.

Over the last 10 years, I've tried, tested, and tweaked so many different approaches to planning, but there was always something that didn't feel quite right. I've been teaching quarterly planning to my clients for years at this point, and it's the closest thing I've ever gotten to creating a realistic, doable plan.

For service business owners, focusing on quarterly planning helps you constrain the number of things you put into motion. This is critical when you consider that when you work with clients, you have limited time to work on your business, and you really only need to focus on your marketing, sales, and service.

After all, a service business, especially a solo one, should be simple. Yet, the way planning is marketed and taught to us makes it complicated, wastes time, and can make us feel like we're not doing nearly enough.

Why? Planning is an extremely lucrative subset of the "products for entrepreneurs" industry, and the natural extension of hustle culture where we want to always try to do more and make more.

Planning has value, but this relentless "new year, new you" and "best year ever" messaging which is designed to sell planners, workshops, calendars, apps, masterminds, and coaching, creates a feeling that we need to buy something and spend a pile of time planning to succeed.

In my experience, most planning products provide cookie cutter solutions to societal-level challenges. No planner is going to help you magically fix the fact that you're in a season of life where you're caregiving for a sick parent, and no app will unlock the key to building wealth. These solutions only provide temporary relief as you feel more in control, but they simply don't offer what most of us need to make lasting changes.

As a solo, service business owner, you need a practical approach to planning that recognizes you have limited time to work on the business, and that you're doing it as a team of one.

Shulamit Ber Levtov encourages entrepreneurs to consider business planning and processes as a form of mental health support: "By bringing some predictability and structure to your business, you reduce the mental load that results from the constant pressure of making decisions when you don't have a plan."

COMMON PLANNING CHALLENGES

Before you think I hate all things planning, know that I actually love planners. I love all the accessories and a fresh set of Zebra pens to write in my planner. I'm a sucker for year-on-the-wall calendars, and even planning books and podcasts.

But friends, despite my love for these things and my being convinced it may fix my life and business, it never has.

Planning is a necessary business activity but not a magical fix, so we need to watch for these potential challenges.

Does This Fit Your Life?

You started a business to support your life, yet so many entrepreneurial planning solutions separate the two. You need your business goals to be compatible with your personal needs.

Your life goals should come first and not be put on hold for your business. No goal is worth pursuing at the expense of your joy and happiness. No revenue goal or business accomplishment will be worth achieving if it's at the expense of the rest of your life.

A couple of years ago, Emily Gertenbach, the content writer we met in Chapter 3, found herself with a goal that was all wrong for her: "I set an income goal that was way too high, and I burned out very, very quickly. A few weeks into my new client load, I was in the car with my husband, zoned out due to fatigue and mental burnout. I turned to him and said I'd made a big mistake. I ended up having to let some clients go later that year as I was having a hard time functioning. The extra money just wasn't worth it."

Does This Fit Your Business?

Too many times, planning approaches or tools are one-size-fits-all, and they aren't right for the type of business you run.

As a service business, you need an approach that recognizes that you're working on your business goals and supporting your clients. As a solo business owner, you also need an approach that recognizes you don't have a team of 12 people to help make this happen.

You need a fundamentally different approach based on your type of business and the ability to hyperfocus on the core areas that will actually move things ahead.

For solo business owners, you need to make a habit of challenging yourself about what you decide to prioritize. Does it align with your overall business strategy? How does it contribute to specific needs around your marketing, sales, and service?

Don't mistake a vanity project for a strategic one. Something that doesn't actually contribute to your business in a meaningful way is busywork; that time would be better spent elsewhere.

"I was trying to keep up with the Joneses," says Deborah Enriquez, a bookkeeping strategist. "I attempted to model my company after others. It took me a while to realize that the company I want to work for is the one that "I" need to envision and build, not someone else's version of it. From my tech stack to my workflows, it has to be what works for me and how I work. Not someone else's idea of what I should do."

Does This Work For You?

Just like a planning process may not work for your business, it may not work for you. You must ensure that any goals or priorities you set align with your unique needs, how your brain works, your values, your work style, your strengths, and more.

Women's leadership coach Susan B. Bentley found that setting annual goals was completely wrong for her: "I've never kept to them or achieved them because of my very real issues with time and ADHD! Now, I set seasonal goals and don't beat myself up if I don't achieve them."

It's not up to me to tell you what goals are right (or wrong) for you, but I challenge you to question if the planning and goal setting you're doing is aligned with your needs. There's simply no point in you planning or working towards goals that are going to make you hate your business or are needless busywork.

Does This Waste Time?

I get it. Planning is fun. And it feels like you're doing meaningful work. It can calm you down when you're worked up. (Trust me, I do all of these things.)

But we can use it as an avoidance mechanism for doing the actual work. We can stall out on making progress on our goals by procrastinating.

I'm 100% guilty of this procrasti-planning, and being aware of my tendency to do this forces me to check in on *why* I want to plan. Do I really need to plan, or is something else going on entirely?

On the flip side of procrasti-planning is planning in a way that has you in hot pursuit of far too many priorities. When working as a consultant and mentor for service-based business owners, I encourage those clients to focus on a maximum of three priorities for a three-month period, as that's realistically what they can focus on.

It's far better to bring one or two goals across the finish line than to have 12 that are only 10% in progress.

> Ultimately, discernment is the key to planning as a solo business owner. You need to have the discipline to prioritize only what's aligned with you and your business's needs. And any goals you set must be tightly aligned with your business strategy, focusing on marketing, sales, and service.

SHIFTING TO SEASONAL PLANNING

Something I've come to loathe is the big end-of-year push on planning that's all about making the coming year the most magical year you've ever had. Talk about pressure!

This approach is fundamentally flawed as it puts so much focus on a one-time event and not nearly enough focus on the process.

Planning shouldn't be static. Planning is an ongoing process in your business, especially as life happens, business evolves, and you sometimes even change your mind. So when you think about planning, you need to consider the ongoing care and feeding of your plan and goals.

Which brings me to the concept of seasons. I've been doing quarterly planning for years now, and it's really and truly been the only style of planning that has ever stuck. It's given me enough room to have living, breathing plans within the business so I can test and tweak as I go.

The biggest struggle with this type of planning is that I've followed the calendar year to determine my quarters. What would happen is that I'd be on track for two quarters of the year, then I'd struggle through the other two.

Eventually, I recognized that I needed to do a better job of being realistic about what I could do during certain times of the year. Otherwise (especially in Q1), I would end up feeling worse than I already did while dealing with seasonal depression.

When I decided to adjust my quarterly planning to align with the seasons, I noticed many of my clients doing this naturally as well. As humans, we're much more attuned to the actual seasons than the seemingly arbitrary quarters on a calendar.

Psychologists have studied the impact of seasons on our minds and bodies, and our change in physiological functions. A study from Meyer (2016) examined the "complex impact of seasons on human brain function."

In the study, participants completed two tasks, a sustained attention task and a working memory task: "For the sustained attention task, the maximum and minimum responses were located around summer and winter solstices, respectively, whereas for the working memory task, maximum and minimum responses were observed around autumn and spring equinoxes."

This highlights what they called "process-specific seasonality" in how our brains function, and that's just one example of the seasonal changes we're managing on an ongoing basis. The seasons also impact our sleep, blood pressure, eating patterns, and more, all of which affects how we're functioning on a day-to-day basis. Adjusting to seasonal cycles simply makes sense as it accounts for what we're really experiencing at different times of year.

Naturally, this data should be applied differently in the Southern hemisphere or in areas of the world that don't experience seasonal changes.

Today, as a Canadian who experiences all four seasons, my planning is built purely around the four seasons, with two seasons very focused on the business — Spring (Mar/Apr/May) and Fall (Sept/Oct/Nov) — and two seasons that are more chill business-wise — Summer (Jun/Jul/Aug) and Winter (Dec/Jan/Feb).

You don't have to align around the seasons specifically or you may not live in a place that experiences all four seasons. It's more about having the freedom to shift your planning and more importantly goals in a way that honors the season you're currently in.

The best part is that as a solo business owner, you can find the way that works *best* for you and you don't have to stick to one rigid formula. Watch for the natural cycles in your life and business, and plan accordingly, even if it's not aligned with the calendar!

WHAT SEASON ARE YOU REALLY IN?

Years ago, I heard the term "season of sacrifice" on the podcast *Happier in Hollywood*, and I always think about it.

Not because we should be constantly sacrificing ourselves to our business, but rather because we need to recognize what season we may be in, either in our business or life, at any given time.

That may sound obvious, but in my personal experience and working with my clients, most of us aren't good at this. We want to adopt a "business as usual" approach and keep on truckin'.

That approach will work until it doesn't; truthfully, it often makes us feel like shit about our business. In a world that's obsessed with the next milestone or revenue goal, it's far too easy to tell yourself that you can get through it if you just buckle down or do this one thing.

But what happens when you just can't white-knuckle your way through and make your plans a reality? You feel like you're failing.

Your goals, plans, and business need to adjust to the season you're in. Especially as a team of one. You're a limited resource, and the last thing you want to do is hustle your way through and drive yourself into a state of complete and utter burnout.

If you're wondering what types of seasons you may encounter, there are too many to count. I've dealt with so many different seasons both personally and professionally, and being willing to embrace the season — good, bad, or seriously ugly — meant I was able to adjust as needed. Sometimes these were life events, professional challenges, or even personal decisions where I was feeling some kind of way.

This is why I encourage clients to proactively identify what season they're in with their business.

Striving

This is a season where you're working consistently towards a specific goal or focused on overall growth in the business.

Sustaining

Part of building a sustainable business is knowing when you're in a season where you need to simply maintain what you've built. You can't strive in every single season indefinitely.

Slowing

Sometimes there are seasons when you need to strategically slow down with your business to prioritize other parts of your life. Slowing means you're reducing speed, so you can speed up at a later date.

The best part is that you get to choose, and the seasons always change. Another one will come soon enough and you can choose something new.

Your seasons are temporary, so what if you decided to work with them instead of resisting? What if you decided to use them strategically to help you create realistic plans instead of trying to box yourself into an arbitrary version of what your business should look like right now?

That's the approach that more solo business owners need and less of this big box hyped-up celebrity-entrepreneur-style planning.

HOW TO PLAN PRACTICALLY

I work closely with my clients on their planning, and in all honesty, I don't care if they plan seasonally, quarterly, monthly, or whatever. The key is that they're doing planning in an increment that enables them to be strategic about what they're working on.

No matter what season you're in — striving, sustaining or slowing — having a plan is about ensuring you're not just checking things off on an endless to-do list. That's a one-way ticket to burnout, and my goal is to help you have a business that's truly sustainable.

In the sustainable approach, you need to constrain the number of goals you set in any given season. Trying to prioritize too many items at one time leads to having no real priorities, and makes it less likely you'll get anything accomplished.

I typically recommend limiting the number of goals or priorities to three, and my clients love to challenge me on this. The harsh truth is that we have constrained time to make progress on these goals. When our attention is divided between too many areas, we lack focus and are less likely to see tangible wins.

My thinking around this has been heavily influenced by the book *The 12 Week Year* by Brian Moran. While aspects of this approach don't apply to us as service business owners, the concept of *periodization* is incredibly relevant.

Periodization is used by athletes to break training into smaller increments, and is similar to the idea of sprints from the Scrum process used in corporate settings to achieve a specific goal in a set amount of time. The idea is that by working in a shorter time frame with more focus, you're able to build momentum faster.

Instead of working on an annual plan with 10 or more goals, you're selecting between one and three to work on for each season or quarter. While this approach has the potential to lapse into the territory of trying to be hyper productive, it ensures you're working on what matters most.

In my experience, most service business owners will create a laundry list of all the things they'd like to do with little discernment about what matters, and forget about the rest of their lives. Quickly, you may find that you're not able to accomplish what you'd planned and feel frustrated or bad about it.

I know the word "practical" is not exciting or sexy, but when it comes to planning, it's a must. Practical planning enables you to feel good and actually get things done on a realistic timeline.

YOUR LIFE COMES FIRST

Your goals need to fit your life, so when doing any business planning, you need to start by taking a look at what's going on in your life. If you're in a busy season personally or have a big vacation planned, you may want to dial back your business plans and have a slow season for it.

As a reminder, there's no separating your business from your life, and you started your business to support your life, so you need to plan in a way that's enabling you to thrive every single day.

The first step in your planning process should always look at what commitments you have for the upcoming season:

- What personal commitments do you already have?
- What personal commitments do you need to make?
- Do you have time off planned?

I always encourage my clients to set personal goals before anything else. Sometimes, those are goals that focus on specific events or needs; in other cases, it's about building daily habits like taking a lunch break, ending work early, or getting into a good sleep routine.

Big or small, life comes first, and your business has to support whatever you need in every season.

SETTING BUSINESS GOALS THAT MATTER

One of the reasons I talk so much about planning with clients is that setting goals is easy, but setting goals that actually matter is much, much more challenging.

As a service business owner, the key is focusing on three core areas of your service business: marketing, sales, and service. When considering what goals to set for your business, focusing on these three areas helps ensure that you're committing to activities that you care about.

After all, marketing, sales, and service are what lead to healthy growth in a business that works with clients. Anything else has the potential to be busywork or a complete waste of your valuable time.

Thinking about your business and where you're heading next, consider these questions to help map out your goals:

- What areas of my business need time and attention?
- Is there anything new I need to add? Anything I need to change?
- Do I have the number of clients I need coming through the door?
    - If not, what do I need to be working on to increase that number?
    - If yes, what do I need to do to ensure that continues?
    - Is there anything I need to change or update?

- How are my sales? Is there anything I need to focus on?
    - What specific area needs work?
    - Where am I feeling friction or struggling with sales?
    - What is my close rate and do I need it to be higher?

- What's the current state of my services?
    - Are there areas for improvement? If so, what needs focus?
    - What kind of feedback am I getting from my clients?
    - Do I feel like I'm missing any elements of the process?

Keep in mind that your goals can build over time, so you don't need to do all of this at once. Start small, and build from there in subsequent seasons. Most of all, don't overthink it to the point that you take no action. Having one crystal clear goal is much better than having no goals at all.

MAKING YOUR PLAN HAPPEN

Next, let's talk about how you're going to make those goals happen. If you take the time to actually set your goal, you need a way to ensure you can follow through.

Once your goals are set, get out your calendar and set aside time to work on the business. To make tangible progress, you can't just squeeze it in around your client work.

Something that's worked well for many of my clients is setting aside a half-day per week, or a day once a month that's fully committed to working on their goals. Honestly, the *amount* of time isn't the important part; it's that you have time to *execute* on tasks related to the goals.

The second part of this exercise is taking each goal and brain dumping all the decisions and tasks needed to get from idea to reality. This will help you ensure that when you sit down to work on these goals you're not spending time trying to decide what to do, or figuring out what you were even trying to do.

Keep in mind that this is an ongoing process, and you'll learn over time what works best for you.

REVIEWING YOUR GOALS REGULARLY

Part of your planning process is actively assessing how it's going. Set aside time each week or month to review your progress on the plan. This can be a simple 10- or 15-minute exercise where you check in so you can calibrate and course correct.

As you get into action, you'll have insights that impact the original goals. You may decide to break a goal in two or alter it in some way. Rest assured, this is completely normal, and all part of the process.

Use these questions to review your goals with curiosity and zero judgement:

- What did I achieve?
- What went well?
- What did I learn?
- How did I do overall?
- What may need to be updated?
- What lessons am I bringing with me?

PLANNING IS AN ONGOING PROCESS

As we wrap up this chapter on planning, I want to remind you that planning isn't an event; it's an ongoing process. How you choose to plan may change over time, but it's an important and necessary business activity, especially as a team of one.

It's really easy to decide that, as it's just you in your business, you don't need to do any planning, but trust me, it's an essential part of being able to build a sustainable business.

To help you with your planning, you'll find a seasonal planning workbook in the Staying Solo Starter Kit. You can sign up for free at www.stayingsolokit.com.

Chapter 7

WHAT SUPPORT DO YOU REALLY NEED?

S olo doesn't mean alone. One of the biggest mistakes I think any business owner can make is deciding that they're on their own and that they don't need support.

In the online business world, there are two distinct types of support that are pushed as the best way to build and grow your business. First, you need a coach to give you the blueprint for your business. Second, you need to hire a team.

But let's be real. That's some oversimplified BS that's doing far too many service business owners a disservice. And as usual, this narrative exists in order to — you guessed it — sell you stuff.

The perpetual stream of ways to get "support" for your business can be overwhelming and confusing. In this chapter, we'll look at how to make intentional and strategic decisions about why and when to get support.

ENTREPRENEURIAL LONELINESS IS REAL

As a service business owner, you're actively supporting your clients. I don't have to tell you that a lot goes into providing services to clients on a day-to-day basis. On top of that, you're running your business and living your life, all of which takes time, energy, skill, and so much more.

When I work with solopreneurs, I can see a sigh of relief that happens once we get into the groove. Usually, they've been on their own for so long, it's refreshing to have someone in their corner who understands both them and their business.

I can absolutely relate. For years, I had very limited support in my business.

Frankly, I didn't recognize how much I was carrying along until I did. And then I signed up for support in spades! That's not to say all the support I've had in that time has been great. When I entered the fray and started seeking some people to support me, I hired some really terrible coaches. I also made some ridiculous decisions based on what I thought I "should" be doing.

But when I've had great support (from a variety of places which we'll dive into a moment), it made a marked difference as I didn't feel like I was all by myself with my business.

The fact is, owning a business can be stressful, but it can also be incredibly lonely. A 2016 study by Fernet, a researcher and professor at the Universite de Quebec, and colleagues looked at the phenomenon of entrepreneurial loneliness and how it contributes to burnout. The research found that the more lonely owners were, the more likely they were to burn out, as they were deeply invested in the company at the expense of connection.

Robert S Weiss is considered one of the foremost experts on loneliness, and his 1973 research

said that "loneliness is caused not by being alone but by being without some definite needed relationship or set of relationships."

Shulamit Ber Levtov, the therapist we met in Chapter 5, works with entrepreneurs to provide mental health support and says that isolation is one of the most common challenges we all face:

"The loneliness of holding space for our clients is about being surrounded by people and having to hold space for them by (appropriately) putting your own self aside, but who holds space for you in that case? You're alone with it all. The perceived need for impression management can hamper our willingness to share enough with others to be able to connect with them, so we can feel lonely because of that disconnection."

She goes on to share that, "Evidence links perceived loneliness and social isolation with depression, poor sleep quality, impaired executive function and cognitive decline. It's easy to see why this is a challenge to business owners and to their businesses."

In the same way that we need a social support system, we need a support system within our business. We need various types of relationships so that we are *not* going it alone.

This doesn't automatically mean you need to hire a virtual assistant or join a high-ticket program. As a solo business owner, you need support that's going to work in conjunction with your unique needs and in service of your goals.

Support is Crucial to Your Mental Health

Ber Levtov works with entrepreneurs and has built her practice around the concept of "being stronger with support," because support is crucial to your mental health.

She shared with me that there are "many aspects of mental health support that we wouldn't think of as mental health support," such as having a trusted contractor or assistant, peer support, formal emotional support, business consulting, and even boundaries and business planning processes.

Ber Levtov says entrepreneurs need to ensure "control for the mental health risks, just as you would for any other risk in business, by making care for your mental and emotional well-being an integral part of your business planning and processes."

Remember the research I shared in Chapter 5 from Freeman and associates about the prevalence of mental health issues in entrepreneurs? With 72% of participants self-reporting mental health issues including depression and substance abuse, this isn't a risk we should be willing to ignore.

The many stressors and negative events in business ownership can lead to mental health struggles. As Ber Levtov explains, "If you don't address their impact, your capacity is compromised. As an entrepreneur, your brain and mind is your greatest asset, and if you're not functioning well, your ability to run your business will be hampered. Better functioning leads to better decision making along with more ease, a more profitable business and more satisfied customers."

In the context of getting support, she encourages us to remember that we're all human: "There doesn't need to be a reason or an argument to legitimize care for yourself. Humans are worthy of care. You are worthy of care."

WHAT TYPE OF SUPPORT DO YOU NEED?

One of the reasons I started BS-Free Business in 2016 is that I was sick and tired of being unable to find the type of business support I wanted. While I'd been fortunate enough to have several reliable and trusted business friends as well as contractors/collaborators, I found myself struggling with two key things.

First, I wanted a mentor who knew what it was like to build a service business. I'd joined masterminds, worked with coaches, and been a part of programs — all with mixed results. Some of the support I received was super helpful, but after a while, I needed something more specific to the type of business I was building. And in other cases, the person I was looking to for guidance didn't give a flying fig about me or my business.

Secondly, I was fortunate in 2013 to join a community that was full of some of the best people I've met business-wise. I'm still friends with many of those people today. The only problem was that I needed something more specialized as a service business owner, as I didn't want to talk about Facebook ads or growing my email list.

Honestly, this messed with me, as I started to think it was a me-problem. I wondered if I was wrong to be all-in on having a service-based business. This thinking resulted in wasted time, money, and effort.

Ultimately, it was my business friends who saw things clearly and told me (and my then-business-partner) to create what we wanted for ourselves.

I've shared parts of this story before, but the more time passes, the more I realize how much all the external chatter and input from coaches who didn't get it did a real number on my confidence. I'm so grateful to those business friends who cut the BS and gave me the push they did.

Years later, I'm glad I pursued the service business route, as supporting other service business owners has been one of the most rewarding things I've ever done. Maybe it's because I know the frustration of feeling alone or unsupported on your business journey. Or the questioning when you wonder if you're missing something.

No matter what the structure of my business has been over the last 20 years, support has been the one constant. I'm incredibly grateful. The reality is you suffer and so does your business when you feel unsupported.

That's one of the reasons I included support as one of the six pillars of the Staying Solo® Framework.

Support comes in so many different shapes and forms, so it's not enough to decide you need support of *some kind*. You need to get specific.

A lack of clarity about what type of support you're seeking can easily contribute to making "investments" that are misaligned.

Celebrity entrepreneurs make big promises that are incredibly enticing when you're seeking support for your business. In many cases, they weaponize your desire for support, connection, and community, and use it against you to make the sale.

In my 2023 Online Business Investment Survey, respondents shared their frustration with false promises, and the general bait and switch of these offers. In short, claims would say anything to make the sale. The marketing for so many types of support sounds good, but it's critical that you slow down and consider what you *really* need.

Generally, support that most solopreneurs would need falls into one of four categories.

Business Solutions 💼	Skills Acquisition 📖	Community Connection 👥	Personal Support 💝
Professional Services	Programs	Masterminds	Therapist
Consulting	Courses	Networking communities	Health professionals
Strategist	Certifications	Social media connections	Family and friends
Coaching	Free resources	Business friends	Support at home
Done-For-You			Apps
Advisory products			
Tech platforms and apps			

Start by clarifying what category you need help in and the type of help that exists in that category. I often see people doing skills development when they don't have time for it and would be better served by hiring a done-for-you service provider. Another common one is enrolling in a course or program with a community attached as a way to build relationships.

Also, please avoid the temptation to rack up certifications as you feel like you need more training. In recent years many faux experts have launched certifications which do little to advance your business and are simply a cash grab.

If you're not sure what support you may need, start with these questions:

- Do I want to learn how to do this, or have it done for me?
- Am I looking for help with strategy or tactics?
- Do I need business-specific support or more personal support?
- How much time and energy do I want to spend on this?
- Do I have a budget for this?
- What type of skills or experience should my "support" have?

- What are my expectations for this support?
- What would make this a win?

PICK THE RIGHT SUPPORT AT THE RIGHT TIME

Remember when I talked about how I tried so many different things on my quest to get business support? You may have identified with that feeling of trying out other solutions but not getting what you're after.

I attribute that to a lack of understanding of what support could look like, along with a constant barrage of "solutions" that play on our fears and insecurity. As I've mentioned, most of the solutions offering support in the online business world are coaching, courses, or programs.

Hiring a coach when you need a therapist or joining another course when you need a consultant will likely lead to discontentment and possibly resentment. If you're seeking out support, getting the wrong type of support can do more harm than good, so we need to be able to look critically at what we truly need.

For example, ADHD coach Amelie Leveille recommends that business owners with ADHD get help with tasks that are hard for them to do: "Trying to become good at things you're not isn't a good use of your time. Focus on what you're good at."

Honestly, her advice is applicable to all business owners. If you're not good at math, trying to do your own books is likely going to create needless stress and procrastination, and cost you far more than it saves in the long run.

When you look at the definition of support, it means a lot of different things, but the one I like in the context of business is "to give courage, faith, or confidence to help or comfort." That's the type of support we all need!

Also, the root of the word "support" is *port*, which means *to carry*. When looking for support, consider where you need help carrying. Support is about helping you carry the load in some way.

That will be dramatically different for each one of us, but being able to nail down exactly where we need help will make all the difference. Here are specific areas to consider when it comes to support.

Services-Based Support

Naturally, when we think of services that may support us, we think of coaching. I fully believe there's a time and place for coaching, but it's a mistake to hire a coach when you need an accountant, lawyer, or brand strategist.

Sometimes, you need support in doing something and taking action (which is what a coach will help you do). Sometimes, you need someone to just do it for you. Services such as consulting, professional services, strategists, or other done-for-you services can help support you by alleviating part of your load with their expertise.

Going back to the scenario above of doing your own books, there's a reason that was the very first thing I outsourced in my business. I knew full well it would cause me immense stress to handle bookkeeping or attempt any type of accounting, so I made it a priority in my business. The same goes with editing my podcasts. I've been podcasting for 10+ years and have never edited a single episode as it's simply a non-negotiable for me.

Skills-Based Support

Most of us don't start a business with all the skills we need to run that business, so periodically, we need support to help us build our competence and capabilities. That may be a program, course, or certification that we pay for. Or it could be a book or a free resource.

When assessing skills-based support, take the time to be *very* clear on what skills you actually need and how they will move your business forward. Don't fall into the trap of taking an expensive 12-month certification to chase a money-making opportunity when you could take a $50 pricing workshop and make more money immediately.

Also, remember, just because something costs a lot does not mean it's better quality or will give you superior support.

I answer a lot of questions from my clients about whether they should pursue different opportunities to expand their skills, and my question always comes back to what their goals are. Consider if you actually need to grow your skills, or if there's potentially something else at play such as a need for more practice or a lack of confidence.

Community Support

Community is about fellowship and having things in common. Maybe it's where you live, the type of business you run, your interests, or any number of items. In the online world, community has become a bit of a catch-all for "you've all paid for this thing, and I'm going to throw you in a Facebook group." That's in no way a true community.

Community-based support is powerful, but you need to have a shared purpose, along with a commitment to supporting one another for real. One of my favorite things in the mastermind communities we run is seeing people genuinely invested in one another's success and helping each other.

Community support can come in many forms, from masterminds to networking communities to social media to your business friends. The key is having that common connection and purpose, as well as an understanding of how you work together.

Using myself as an example, community has been a cornerstone of my business for over 10 years. It's the reason you're reading this book! It took two friends telling me it was finally time, then countless people in my community sharing their stories and experiences, to help this book become a reality.

At the risk of sounding cheesy, the community formed through my business has been a lifeline over the years with everything from navigating challenging client situations to checking in on me when life happens. I'm incredibly grateful, and I want everyone to have this type of support as a business owner.

Personal Support

Finally, personal support often gets overlooked or is talked about in a way that's completely privileged and infuriating.

I'm not talking about this flippant "hire help" or "outsource your life" type of BS we see on social media where people get all this help so they can hustle harder. What I'm talking about here is having the right structures in place on a personal level so that you have time to do your work and you're able to run your business sustainably.

Personal support will look very different based on your stage of life and your individual and/or family needs. In the early days of my business, I needed the support of a house cleaner and daycare for my tiny human. Today, I need a therapist and health professionals to support me with my mind and body.

Personally, I believe that every business owner can greatly benefit from therapy. While I'd initially gone to therapy to deal with anxiety, complex PTSD, and grief, I ended up exploring many topics that directly related to my business. Entire appointments were dedicated to discussing how to navigate specific situations or even how to reset boundaries.

Whether it's therapy or something else entirely, personal support is key to your business. Sometimes it can be as simple as taking a walk with a friend or family member you can talk to about your business, or restructuring the schedule with your loved ones so you're not working in the evenings.

DIFFERENT SEASONS REQUIRE DIFFERENT SUPPORT

You'll need different types of support in different seasons of your business. The support you need will change and evolve, and no type of support will be the perfect solution forever.

One of my biggest pet peeves in the online business world is the value-ladder type offers that are designed to lock people into an ever-escalating series of investments under the guise of support. That's not the support that you need. That's a thinly-disguised pyramid scheme.

We've been sold this idea that we must have very specific types of support continuously to be "successful," when it's really about continuing to extract money from us. This is one of the cultistic aspects of the online business industry, where we are indoctrinated into being fearful of leaving that ecosystem.

No type of support will be suitable indefinitely. Period.

So as you consider support, think about your season in business or life, and plan accordingly. Shifting and changing your support over time is natural and normal.

The support I need today is very different than it was when I started my business, and has shifted from being more personally focused to more professionally driven.

As a solopreneur, your support system is essential to building and running a sustainable business, so I encourage you to examine what support you need right now and in the future. (And we need to recognize that sometimes no support is a viable option too!)

Do You Need to Pay for Support?

The other thing I want to address is that for support to be helpful and meaningful, it doesn't automatically need to be something you pay for. A pervasive online business myth is how if you don't pay for something you don't value it.

Again, this is designed to convince us that we need to spend our money for something to have value. (And usually, it's backed up by the BS assertion that the more we pay, the more we'll value it, which exists to justify ridiculous high-ticket pricing.)

Over the years, I've had a mix of support that has made an incredible difference to my business. Some of that has been paid, and some of that has been more community-based. One of my closest friends from my PR program has freelanced on and off so we've always talked about business. I have a strong network of business friends and people I'm connected with on social media that I talk to regularly.

Getting support shouldn't automatically require a massive financial investment. That makes it incredibly elitist and frankly inaccessible to the majority of people. Most people don't have $25k to drop on a fluffy six-month mastermind, including one call a month and a two-day retreat. (Don't even get me started on how messed up that is and how it's buying your business friends…)

Speaking of money, if you're going to pay for any kind of support, I recommend you plan and budget for it. That can help you ensure that your critical thinking isn't short-circuited by manipulative marketing and sketchy sales practices in the heat of the moment.

Let the Buyer Beware

Speaking of the cost of support, I want to touch on the fact that the online business world engages in some extremely problematic business practices designed to exploit our human need to rely on others.

Celebrity entrepreneurs know many are lonely and want their businesses to work, so they take advantage. To reach their income goals, they design "solutions" that aren't really about support at all. Then, they fail to deliver as promised. So it's a double whammy where people pay large sums of money and are deeply disappointed.

I raise this issue as I want everyone to get the support they need when needed, but this isn't the way. Your support doesn't have to be spendy, so please ensure you do your due diligence.

If you're considering coaching, programs, or courses, the 2023 Online Business Investment Survey provides some additional insights in terms of what made the difference in business owners feeling satisfied or unsatisfied with their investment.

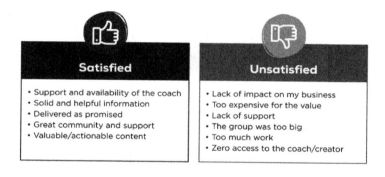

Satisfied	Unsatisfied
• Support and availability of the coach • Solid and helpful information • Delivered as promised • Great community and support • Valuable/actionable content	• Lack of impact on my business • Too expensive for the value • Lack of support • The group was too big • Too much work • Zero access to the coach/creator

If you're looking for more help vetting a potential investment for your business, I encourage you to ask the following questions:

- Is their area of expertise aligned with your needs?
- How long have they been in business?
- How many years of experience do they have doing what they do now?
- Do they support a specific type of business owner or is it more general?

- Are their customers similar to your stage and type of business?
- What does this offer include?
- Does it align with your preferred learning style?
- Are their testimonials specific and believable?
- Do you identify with the people in these testimonials?
- Can you comfortably afford this right now?
- Are their values in alignment with yours?

These questions may seem like overkill, but in the current climate in the online business world, they're completely necessary. For several years, I've been co-hosting a consumer advocacy podcast called *Duped*, which explores the dark side of online business. Through that podcast, I've shared the countless stories I've heard about people investing in support only to get burned.

In the 2023 survey I mentioned above, people opened up how they felt about their worst investments and used words like "regret," "angry," "manipulated," "disgusted," and "shame" to describe the aftermath.

That's why, before you invest in any support, particularly if it's coaching, consulting, courses, or anything else in the online world, you need to do a thorough job of vetting anyone you consider working with.

SUPPORT MAKES YOUR BUSINESS MORE SUSTAINABLE

Being a solo business owner doesn't mean you need to do it alone. If you want to have a truly sustainable business that doesn't lead to burnout, or leave you wanting to burn it all down regularly, you need support.

Based on what I shared in this chapter, consider what type of support you may need in this season of your business. There's no right or wrong answer about what support to seek; it's just important that you have it.

Chapter 8

Ditching Busywork with Systems

Wherever I talk about systems, I see most solopreneurs' eyes start to glaze over or wander. I get it — when you think of systems, you're thinking of complex and boring "systems" that box you in and kill your spirit.

That's not the type of system we'll talk about here. What we're talking about is a way to save you hours every single week and feel less like you're making it up as you go.

Unfortunately, we've all wasted time setting up systems that don't work or we don't use. It's not unknown for systems to totally derail solopreneurs, draining us financially and energetically — I'm looking at you fancy CRM system I wasted over $25,000 on 10 years ago.

Before we get into a simple approach to systems, and what systems you do (and don't) need, I want to talk about why I included it as part of the Staying Solo Framework.

The definition of a *system*, as defined by the Oxford Dictionary, is a "set of principles or procedures according to which something is done," which typically makes solo business owners feel strongly one way or another. Some love systems. Others feel like it's complete overkill for a team of one.

Either way, I get it. But here's the thing. When you're solo, for you to have the capacity or space to run your business and live your life, you don't need to waste time and energy with busywork.

> **Real talk:** When it comes to running your business, there's only so much you can plan. There are always going to be things along the way that throw you a curveball or result in complete chaos.

That's why you don't need to be expending more time and energy than necessary on the things you can control. And those things, my friend, include your systems.

YOUR SYSTEMS SHOULD BREED SIMPLICITY

When I talk about systems, I don't mean the type of overcomplicated, overblown systems that most celebrity entrepreneurs talk about. I think of those as "big S" systems, and no matter what these people are trying to tell you or sell you, you don't need those kinds of systems to run a sustainable solo service business.

The goal of the systems you need as a solopreneur is to reduce the cognitive load of daily decision-making. Any system should make your life *easier*, not more complicated, complex, or frustrating.

When I talk about systems, I refer to processes that enable you to run your business efficiently and sustainably. Prioritizing sustainability enables you to grow and maintain your business in a way that truly serves you now and for years.

A system you spend too much time, money, or energy on isn't sustainable. You need to be able to use the systems you create. You need your clients to use them. And you don't want to be stuck having to get help with them constantly.

The perfect example is when I "invested" in a high-end email and customer relationship management (CRM) system. It was a complete waste of time, energy, and most of all, money.

The system was *way* too much for what I needed in my business. It was complicated, and I was so frustrated and overwhelmed by it that I had to hire ongoing help to set it up and manage it. The purchase ended up being a $25k mistake over several years, and that's not even getting into the level of stress it caused me as I felt so out of control.

This may be extreme, but it's the perfect example of how something designed to systematize your business can quickly go off the rails. Your systems should be simple and ultimately serve you.

With that, here's what to consider based on if you're a systems person or if you're more systems-resistant.

If You Love Systems	If You're Systems-Resistant
I want to challenge you to ensure you're not creating systems that simply create busywork for you, or worse yet as a way to feel like you're doing meaningful work, but it's not actually all that useful.	You don't have to document every single thing. Your systems are there to support you, not stifle you. I want to challenge you to think about where you spend needless time or space that could be helped with a system.

Confession: I've gone from being systems-resistant to a systems superfan. For many years when people would talk about systems, it would make me roll my eyes. My brain was like, 'That sounds boring and like it's going to stifle my creativity.'

Little did I know I had a lot of systems in place already through my years as a freelancer. These were things that let me run my business efficiently and save time. I just didn't think of those things as systems.

COMPLICATION AND COMPLEXITY: THE ENEMY OF SUSTAINABILITY

Thanks to the industry of entrepreneurship that we discussed in chapter 1, a lot of complication and complexity has been added to running a business. There are so many rules and recommendations that are designed to make us feel like we're not doing things "right."

As we know, unfortunately, complexity exists to sell you a solution. It creates a problem so someone can offer you their course or group program.

While I firmly believe that business owners must develop different skills at different stages, we should remember that a multi-million dollar industry exists to sell us things to build a business. It's an ecosystem full of entrepreneurs selling to other entrepreneurs.

I recognize I'm part of this B2E ecosystem. However, I got here because I was tired of the crappy solutions available in this market and how so many things were seriously overpriced.

For your business to be sustainable, you need systems that support you daily. So often, I see systems that are overkill for the stage or type of business. For example, if you only bring on three or four new clients per year, you likely don't need a fancy dashboard for your lead tracking when a Google Sheet will do.

With an over-engineered process, you spend too much time, money, and energy on it. You may have to hire experts to set it up or manage it. Systems like these can be hard to get our team or our clients to use. You may not use them as you should, as they're clunky or inconvenient.

That's why I want to advocate for sustainable systems. Complexity is not sustainable, and it defeats the point.

Solopreneurs Need Sustainable Systems

For a solo business owner, it's clear that your systems should be simple, but they should also be sustainable.

A sustainable system is one that you actually use and know you can rely on. What makes it sustainable is that it's easy to use and highly repeatable to the point it becomes second nature for you.

What's not sustainable is anything with 13 videos and seven pages of details on how to use the system. That may sound like a joke, but I'm only half joking. This is how systems are taught in the online business world, as they're primarily designed for people with a team and who are focused on scaling, not solopreneurs staying solo.

There are three key elements of a sustainable system.

Creating a system enables you to pre-determine the steps, tools, and templates you'll use. Remember that this doesn't automatically require you to have highly detailed processes for your systems.

When you're focused on staying solo, you don't need systems to train a team or delegate tasks, so simple is the way to go. You shouldn't ever be spending days of your life creating systems.

If you're just getting started, start with the areas that are causing you the most friction. Where are you wasting time? Where do you spend time trying to figure out the steps? Where are you constantly reinventing the wheel?

Watch for annoyance, frustration, and irritation as indicators that those are places you may need a system. Spending even 15 minutes figuring it out and making some decisions about how, when, and why to do it moving ahead can make a critical difference.

As you're creating systems, ask yourself these four questions to ensure the system is simple and sustainable:

- Are the key decisions made in advance for me?
- Can I easily follow or refer to the system?
- Is it something that supports me consistently?
- Will this grow with me?

If you're a solo business owner with no intention of hiring, there's likely no need for you to spend time and energy documenting systems. If you're solo and think you may hire someone to help with that specific system in your business, then add to the documentation over time.

If you're spending days creating systems that aren't going to see the light of day, that's defeating the point. You'd be better served creating the minimally viable version of the system and building it up organically and gradually.

Finally, the most important aspect of the system is that it reduces the cognitive load of having to make decisions and figure things out.

According to Medical News Today, decision fatigue is the "idea that after making many decisions, a person's ability to make additional decisions becomes worse." If every single time you sit down to work on a task you have to make 10 or 20 little decisions to make any progress, you're adding needless work to your plate. Plus, if it's a task you'd rather not do, you're that much more likely to abandon it completely.

Once I figured this out about systems, I could finally wrap my head around them to make my life easier. I used to get so irritated by the push to document every tiny detail when I was a solo business owner.

At that point, I shifted my thinking from "this is annoying" to "this could be helpful" and mapped out systems for key elements of my business. The result was way less time spent on decisions taking up needless space in my brain.

WHERE DO YOU REALLY NEED SYSTEMS?

In exploring where you need systems, I encourage you to focus on the three main areas of your service business: marketing, sales, and service.

These three core areas of your business impact everything you do as they're focused on finding, selling, and serving clients. These are the places that will hold you back from growth and drain you if they consistently need you to make big decisions.

Here are my top recommendations if you're looking for ideas for systems you likely need as a solo service business owner.

In creating systems, I can't emphasize enough that the basics are better. My systems have always been very no-frills, and that's why they work for my brain and business. They enable me to do the work I want to do, tame the chaos, and keep me from decision fatigue.

When deciding on what systems you may or may not need, evaluate how often you do something, or what creates the most friction. There are so many things you could systematize, but if it's something you do once a year, that's a waste of time. Go for things that will have the biggest impact on your day-to-day life.

Consider where you're wasting time or feeling like you're reinventing the wheel every single time. Also, anywhere you feel frustrated is a surefire sign you need to map out your system.

Also, consider where you can better serve your clients with systems. Your client experience can easily be overlooked, but it's likely somewhere you can make ongoing improvements. Never underestimate how improving onboarding or client communications can make your life easier.

Remember that you don't have to have it all perfectly done today; the key is to get the basics covered. Concentrate on making them bite-sized and manageable, and build from there.

Watch for shiny object syndrome and keep your eyes on your own paper. Seeing what someone else is doing, or checking out a hyped-up new tool, is normal as we're all curious, but it can also create complexity. It can be tempting to think you're missing out, but most likely you're not.

If it's not broken, don't waste time on fixing it.

MUST-HAVE MARKETING SYSTEMS

There are two types of solo service business owners I encounter when I talk about marketing. First, there are the marketers. They're always happy to be testing things out in their own business. Then, there's the rest of the world, who would rather do anything but market their business.

No matter which you are, you need systems in place for your marketing so you're not wasting time.

As a service business owner, you likely have very limited spots for new clients on an ongoing basis, so your marketing can be simple. I remind you of this because I'll often talk to people about these tactics and they'll want to add 77 other things. They believe more marketing is better marketing, but that's patently untrue.

The goal is to focus on the tactics that will have the greatest impact in the least amount of time, which is where the must-haves come in. These tactics — and the systems you need to make them happen — should be considered the bare minimum baseline for every type of service business owner, regardless of their target market.

SEO-Focused Website

FACTS: You need a solid web presence so you're findable online. To maximize your online home, you need to have an SEO-focused website. You need to ensure that your target clients can find you when they're looking for answers to questions you can solve or to hire someone who offers what you do.

Search engine optimization, or SEO, can seem daunting, but it's actually a lot simpler than most people realize. If you have an existing site, ensure you have Google Analytics installed so you can see how your site is performing. This will give you a baseline of how your site is currently doing in search.

From there, consider hiring someone to handle basic SEO for your website pages. I recommend finding someone who doesn't make wild promises about what they can do with your website, like getting you ranked on the first page of search engine results.

Once the basics are covered, your SEO system should entail reviewing key website metrics either monthly or quarterly to see how much traffic your site is getting and if you're bringing in potential clients, and adjusting your strategy accordingly.

Referral Plan

Most service business owners build their client roster via referrals. However, it's pretty common for people to be passive about actually getting those referrals.

Every service business owner needs a system for their referrals and to make a habit of asking for them. Being proactive and making it easy for people to refer you is a simple way to reach more potential clients.

First, you need to map out specific steps for your referrals:

- How often do you ask for referrals?
- Who do you ask?
- What is your specific ask?

Then, you need your tools and templates ready to go. For tools, I recommend you use a project management system or calendar to help you keep track of when you should be asking for referrals, and then use a Google Doc or Sheet to keep track of your contacts.

For templates, I recommend you create a series of canned emails you can use to customize for outreach via email.

Remember, the more you systematize, the more likely you'll be to follow through as you can sit down and take an hour once a month versus wasting time figuring out what you're even doing.

Lead Tracking

Your potential clients, or *leads*, are a critical part of your marketing so you need to be tracking this information in detail. It's important to know from my point of view that a lead is a potential client who's expressed interest in working together, not someone who's simply following you on social email or is on your email list. They're prequalified to some degree as you've talked about working together or there's been some type of meaningful activity to turn them from a passive follower into a potential client.

You can set up a simple spreadsheet, but I can't even tell you how many people don't document this information. It's extremely helpful when it comes time to analyze where your clients actually come from so you're spending your time on the highest value marketing activities.

If you don't know that most of your clients come from referrals, you may be wasting time posting daily on social media when you've never actually signed a client thanks to one of your posts.

You'll want to keep track of your leads on a biweekly or monthly basis, and have enough details so that you know the status of your potential clients. You can also use your lead tracker as part of your sales process to determine data like how many clients say yes to working with you vs how many decline. This metric, called your win rate or loss rate *e*, is a great measure of how appropriate your marketing efforts are, and a way to identify potential issues with your sales process.

You can grab a simple lead tracker in the resources that go with this book at www.stayingsolokit.com.

Content Marketing Systems

While I started out as a PR freelancer, I quickly pivoted into content marketing as soon as blogging and email marketing started to rise in popularity.

Content marketing, which is a form of digital marketing where you create and share material online, such as blog posts, podcast episodes, email newsletters, and so on, can be extremely powerful. So what I'm going to say next may be surprising. I don't believe that all service business owners need to do content marketing.

The reality is that you likely have very limited spaces for clients, so if you're consistently booked out using other methods of marketing, you may not need to be creating content.

Ultimately, the decision to use content marketing for your business should come down to:

1. The type of clients you serve. You need to have an audience for your content, so if your target client isn't consuming this type of content, you'll likely have more success using more direct marketing methods.

2. The time you have to commit to creating content. Content marketing is time consuming, and frankly, it's a long game. If you need clients in the short-term, it's unlikely to yield results.

Case in point, I'm forever hearing from people who decide to work with me that they've been listening to the podcast for years. Think about that. They've been following for years, and I don't even know who they are!

Also, remember, you're a service business owner, not a content creator who can focus solely on creating content.

Now, let's talk about content marketing related systems.

Content: Blog or Podcast

For content marketing you'll need some type of "hero" content, such as a blog or podcast. This will act as the anchor for your other content such as social media and email.

As someone who's blogged for over 15 years, and podcasted for over 10 years, I'm the poster child for consistent content creation, and that comes down to having solid systems in place.

At the heart of your content system is mapping out the steps you'll take to create each piece of content, including:

- What steps are required to go from idea to getting it out into the world?
- How often do you publish?
- What's your focus? What topics or themes do you cover?
- Where will you publish?

The next part of your content system is what tools you use. They may evolve over time, but you'll want to dial into these early in the process. For example, for a podcast:

- Where do you write your notes or scripts for each episode?
- Where do you record your podcast?
- What tools do you need to edit the episode?
- Where is the podcast hosted?
- Where do you publish your show notes or accompanying blog post?

In my case, I use Google Docs for drafting scripts, Riverside. fm for recording, a hired podcast editor, a platform manager known as Libsyn which distributes to all major platforms, and the show notes are on our Wordpress website.

Each one of those tools has steps related to using them, as well as templates such as for script development and our blog posts in Google Docs. Everything is lined up and managed via Google Drive, and our project management system.

Email Marketing

Email is definitely still a powerful way to engage and connect with your audience. That said, people's inboxes are crowded so you need to be committed to creating content that they want to read and consider how you will continue to deliver ongoing value.

If you're new to email marketing, start small. A weekly newsletter is a great way to build a habit and expand over time. It's easy to get sucked into creating all kinds of lead magnets and funnels, but until you have a baseline audience, focus on the basics. (Trust me on this one, fancy funnels and the like are busywork you don't need in your life until absolutely necessary.)

The steps, tools, and templates you need for your email marketing may be similar to the ones for your blog or podcast, but you'll want to decide as much as possible in advance so that your time on a weekly, biweekly, or monthly basis is spent on getting the email written and out the door, not floundering about trying to figure out how to send it.

Social Media

As I said about email, I recommend you keep this simple and find your sweet spot platform, which is a platform your potential clients use and that you enjoy using.

Please don't try to be on all the platforms. Focus on one and do that one really well, as social media can be incredibly time-consuming — you're a service business owner, not a full-time creator.

As for your social media systems, this is going to be a matter of trial and error as things may change as platforms evolve. I do encourage you to spend time on a monthly or quarterly basis ensuring that your social media systems are adapted to the latest and greatest.

Ask yourself if you're focused on creating and posting content, or on all the decisions around how to edit a video, tweak an image, or write a caption. Social media is the ultimate time suck, and because it's so public we can spend far too much time trying to make it perfect when it doesn't actually move our businesses forward.

This is just a sample of potential systems for your marketing, and there are many more you could put in place. They are designed to be examples, and the key is that your marketing time is used effectively each and every week.

SLIP UPS AND STRESS: THE CASE FOR A SIMPLE SALES SYSTEM

Let's be real. Solopreneurs rarely tell me they love sales. They tell me it's draining and stressful, and sucks up precious time, energy, and headspace.

Remember, one of the reasons we want to create sustainable systems is to reduce the cognitive load of making decisions. That's exactly why you need sales systems.

Sales systems help save you time and energy related to all aspects of your sales process. No more reinventing the wheel every time you need to have a conversation with a potential client. No more sweating out writing a proposal or sending the follow-up email.

Sales Slip Ups Can Haunt You Later

We make hundreds of decisions every single day. The more decisions we make, the more fatigued we become. As we become overwhelmed or tired, the quality of our decisions declines.

The quality of your decisions may not be a big deal when it comes to what type of salad dressing to pick or which shirt to wear, but when it comes to sales, you want to make high-quality decisions.

Why? Decisions made in your sales process impact so many aspects of your business. Think of a time you decided to quote a price on a call, which was wrong. Or when you scope a project incorrectly, and do hours and hours of work for free.

Seemingly small decisions during your sales process can become big headaches that haunt you later. Essentially, your sustainable sales systems exist to save you from yourself.

Rather than having a full-blown meltdown over potential mistakes in your sales process, put in some effort beforehand to minimize the risk of poor decision-making.

Sales Stress: From Rejection to Resilience

There are multiple steps in the sales process; some may feel squishier or more stressful than others. Those are the ones you likely need systems for!

But before we get into the nuts and bolts of the systems, I want to address a key question about why sales feel so stressful for many.

There are several reasons, but I want to acknowledge the major ones as they may result in resistance or avoiding dealing with sales-related systems.

"What if I'm bad at sales?"

Honestly, you're probably *not* bad at sales. Selling is so much simpler than people realize, but we work in a culture where we're told "sales are hard" and solutions are pushed on us near-daily.

Before I was in the online business world, I'd been making sales for over a decade. It hadn't been a problem until I encountered a person doing a program on selling. Many friends did this program, and I had a major case of FOMO as I was worried I didn't know what I was doing.

That messaging and marketing can erode your confidence, so I encourage you to shut it out and just focus on sorting out your sales systems. That will do more to help you feel confident about your sales skills than any program ever will.

For some, the fear of rejection or worrying you're not good enough may factor into how you feel about sales. I want to remind you that if someone doesn't want to work with you it's not a judgment on you. In fact, if they're engaged in the sales process with you, there must be a reason that they got there in the first place.

Generally speaking, people don't talk to people about potentially working together if they think the person is unqualified and unskilled.

Finally, you may simply be overwhelmed by the process. You may feel like you don't have time to deal with potential clients or to do the work you need to do to get them to say yes.

That's exactly why you need these sales systems in place. The goal is to build sustainable sales systems that help you build resilience around anything that stresses you out about your sales.

SIMPLIFIED SALES SYSTEMS FOR EVERY SERVICE BUSINESS OWNER

Now, let's get down to it and talk about simplifying your sales. Some of these elements may vary depending on what type of services you offer and who your clients are, but I want to talk through a typical sales process.

Packages
What you're selling is the starting point for your sales process. If you offer services, there are countless ways to sell your services, but I highly recommend you have packages.

If you're creating a custom package for every client, you need to cut that out. You're making your sales process more complicated than it needs to be!

Creating a package lets you pre-decide the scope of work, deliverables, and so on, which means you can position your services as a solution to a problem. If you immediately went on the defense and thought, 'but my clients are all so different...', I'm going to challenge you on that. Are they all really that different? You can create different packages for different types of clients. Better yet, you might niche down so that working for anyone and everyone doing everything doesn't make your business harder than it needs to be.

Having packages helps you spend less time in the sales process as you're targeting a specific group of potential clients, so you're not wasting time with people who will never be a fit. Plus, you know exactly how to scope a project out.

Pricing

With your packages developed, you must also have clear and consistent pricing. In terms of systems, you need a pricing strategy in place.

For example, what's the baseline hourly pricing you use to calculate your prices? What are your hard costs? How much markup or padding do you need to include?

These questions may not seem like a "system" per se, but having these ironed out enables you to take a systematic approach to pricing your projects. It removes the emotion or judgment, and helps you ensure you don't underprice yourself.

This may be as simple as having a pricing plan and calculator in place, so you've done this critical thinking in advance.

Consults

You know something I don't like? Awkward conversations with strangers, especially when those strangers are deciding whether or not to work with us. This is why having a system around consults has been a total lifesaver for me.

Instead of getting on Zoom and feeling like the whole thing is totally awkward and then nervously talking to fill the air, I have a structure to follow.

Invest some time deciding in advance everything related to your consults, including:

- Who gets to have a consultation?
- What do they need to do?
- Where do they book?
- How long is the consultation?
- What's the structure of the call?
- Where does it happen?
- What templates, tools, and tech do you need?

Getting that all out of the way lets you take control of the consult call and drive the conversation forward. Plus, you're not wasting time on calls that are going nowhere fast or are just people picking your brain.

Proposals

Next up are proposals. Once you've had that initial conversation with a client, you'll likely be sending them an official invitation to work together called a proposal or sometimes an estimate, pitch, or quote, depending on the detail.

I know that many people hate proposals, so I'm dedicated to singing their praises at every opportunity.

The reason proposals can suck is that you're doing so much of the work at the moment. However, when you rely on a sales system, you have your packages and pricing nailed down, and can put them into the proposal easily. For this, you should have a template with your pricing and wording ready to pop in.

If you do write proposals, for the love of your service business and your sanity, please sit yourself down and create a template.

Aside from a template for your proposals, I recommend creating template emails for sending your proposal and deciding if you want to use any tools. For example, we deliver our proposals for the agency via Proposify. It's definitely a nice-to-have, but it significantly speeds up the process of creating and sending proposals.

Other Sales Tools

Depending on what type of work you do, you may need certain sales tools. For creative work, you might think about a portfolio. For other industries, you may need client references or a one-pager with a summary of your services.

If you're unsure, pay attention to questions you get from potential clients in the sales process. That often is a sign of friction, and you may need something else to help them decide.

We often send our portfolio to potential clients before a call, or as part of a proposal. As a result, we ensure it's up to date and ready to go at a moment's notice.

With business to business (B2B) tech companies, we're occasionally asked for references from current or past clients, so I have specific people I know are okay with us giving out their contact info.

And finally, sometimes, in the early stages of sales engagement, people need a summary of services with some baseline pricing, so that's where the one-pager comes in.

What tools you need may vary, but as you consider your sales process, you may need specific supporting elements.

Closing Clients

You're nearly there, and you're waiting for a yes. And waiting. And waiting.

The proposal has been sent, you've answered the follow-up questions, and nothing. So what do you do next?

This is where you need a closing system, which can be as simple as a set of emails following up with potential clients at set intervals. You can simply write the emails in advance and set reminders for you to send them out. That helps make it a task to handle versus something that sucks up energy because you don't know what to do, so you do nothing.

Fumbling the follow-up can mean the difference between a yes and a big fat nothing. So with a little setup, you can close more new clients.

TAME THE CLIENT SERVICE CHAOS

We've all been there. We're overwhelmed and ready to burn it all down if one more client asks you one more question. It's chaos, and you're out of capacity for any of it.

When you started your service business, if you're like most people, it's because you had specific skills and experience. You may do creative or consulting work or have worked in an agency or a non-profit, but it doesn't automatically mean you have the countless skills required to serve clients.

We don't think of these as skills, but they really are. In my case, I've been building them for over 20 years, so I've got the benefit of a lot of trial and error.

From payments to communications to project management and everything in between, there are many moving parts with serving clients. All of which require skills, systems, and, ultimately, our brain power.

Whether we started a business knowing how to do them or not, all of those parts are critical to our business and our success. How we manage our clients can make or break our business.

Think about the last time you had a bad customer service experience. It feels awful when you're on the receiving end, and it can lead to losing trust or even not doing business with that company again.

I'm not talking about a client who has turned into the client from hell, but rather one where you didn't have the skills or systems in place and chaos reigned supreme. Where things got away from you and the relationship went sour.

This may be the quality of work slipping, a lack of professionalism, or poor communication. All of these, especially if they add up over time, can lead to the end of a client relationship.

A customer experience study from consulting firm PWC found that in the U.S. 17% of customers will walk away after one bad experience and 59% after several bad experiences.

As microbusinesses, we can prevent these types of experiences from ever happening. Investing in our client experience is good for business too since it costs between five and 25 times more to find a new customer than to keep an existing one.

By being proactive with our customer service, we can retain our clients, expand our relationships, and have them happily refer us.

As someone with long-standing retainer client relationships, focusing on client service has always been my top priority and my best growth strategy.

I can point to multiple client examples where, by building that relationship and providing great service, we could 2x or 3x the size of the original monthly retainer.

It's Not Time Management; It's Capacity

By now, you're probably thinking of a cringe client situation where you dropped the ball. I get it. It's happened to me, and frankly, it's embarrassing. It feels like crap, even when I think about it years later.

So before we talk about specific systems to have in place to deal with your client service, I want to acknowledge that you're human. You have limited resources as a business owner and, as we've already seen, limited capacity.

We often think of client service challenges as being the result of needing more time. The bigger issue is our limited capacity to track everything, make decisions, and communicate daily. (This is a big reason I encourage my clients to limit their number of clients at any given time.)

When you have a full (or overfull) client roster, a brain that can only hold so much info, a life to live, and you don't want to work around the clock, something's got to give.

That's why systems are so crucial. The right client service systems help you maximize your capacity by removing the ongoing emotional, energetic, and cognitive load of these activities.

Yes, you have to do them, but you're no longer spending your time obsessing over how you're doing them, trying to reinvent the wheel, or procrastinating on doing them because you're not sure where to start.

Having client service systems helps you proactively prevent problems before they even start. And it forces you to be much more realistic about what you can commit to and get done in a given day, week, or month.

ELIMINATING COMMON CHALLENGES THROUGH CLIENT SERVICE SYSTEMS

Next, let's discuss what systems you need for client service. Some of these you may already have in place, some you may need help with, and others you may not even look at as a system.

When you think about systems, I want you to forget the 73-page standard operating procedure (SOP) or fancy complicated BS, and return to basics. Remember, your system simply pre-determines when and how you'll do something, the tools you need, and the templates required.

That's it. Simple is sustainable when it comes to your systems.

My favourite client service systems are the ones that anticipate potential issues and eliminate them from day one.

One of the hardest parts of running a service business is that we're imperfect humans working with other imperfect humans. You can't assume your clients know how to work with you or even what you expect from them. My policy is to leave nothing to chance and communicate constantly.

With that, let's look at a few common challenges that can be addressed with systems.

Payment Problems

You likely don't think of payments as a system, but it's the top client service system to have for your business. You will have to clearly plan how, when, and where you take payments and what the expectations are. You'll also need to communicate that from day one with potential clients. Payment policies and procedures take the messiness out of potentially awkward client situations, as they are factual, e.g. "We take payment via ACH and invoice on the 25th of the month."

Client Has a Case of the What Abouts

This is one of my least favourite client situations. This is where the client is nagging you about a deadline, the status of an item, or something else. This usually comes down to the client not having a clear line of sight into where things are, which can be fixed with a project management system and a communications system so they're clear on the status, timeline, or deadline.

You can cut this off at the pass by being proactive, so they're not left wondering. This is a great place where a regular communication cadence is required, so they know what's up. Even if you think they should know, overcommunicating with clients is always better.

Mismatched Expectations

Maybe you've got a client who wants to "jump on Zoom" all the time, or they expect a response to their message in your project management system within the hour. I'm the first to admit that expectations can be tricky, so this is a matter of having a clear set of boundaries (aka the rules of client engagement) that are communicated in your onboarding and then reinforced consistently.

These are just a few examples of some of the most common places where clients can push our buttons. With some planning, though, we can have a system in place to be as proactive as humanly possible. Plus, having a system helps protect us from making exceptions and enables us to reinforce how we work with clients when needed.

WHAT CLIENT SERVICE SYSTEMS DO YOU NEED?

If you're thinking about what systems you need in your service business, here are just a few of the must-haves:

- Payments/invoicing
- Onboarding
- Calendar/call management
- Project management
- Ongoing communications
- Offboarding

For each of these, you can make the key decisions so there's a clear plan for the what, when, and how. This can be as simple as a one-page Google Doc with the key questions answered, details on the tools used, and links to any templates you may have created.

For your tools, I encourage you to keep them simple. So many amazing platforms can be a huge waste of time and money if they don't work for you or your clients. Automation has a time and place, but if you spend more time on managing the system than actually saving time with it, it's probably more hassle than it's worth.

BUST THE BS BUSYWORK WITH SYSTEMS

One of the most challenging parts of running a service business is that it's a very simple business model. As a result, you can feel like you're always missing something, so you find ways to fill that gap.

The beauty of the service business model is that you don't need to do those things. You're not missing a thing if you have your basic systems covered.

Your systems help you eliminate busywork so don't go out there and create more of it for yourself.

Successfully staying solo comes down to embracing the simplicity of the service business and focusing on making it sustainable for you. You don't need any of those "secrets" and you're not missing a damn thing. Small, simple, regular actions build a sustainable solo business that lasts.

Chapter 9

Using Strategy to Break the Income Ceiling

One of the biggest frustrations faced by service business owners who want to stay solo is that they feel like they're eventually going to hit an income ceiling.

If you're not familiar with the concept of an income ceiling, it's essentially when you can't make any more money because you've hit the limit of what you can charge and the number of clients you can serve.

On the surface, it's a very simple concept. You only have so many hours in the day and may find there's only so much you can raise your prices for your client base.

The concept of the income ceiling has been used heavily in marketing by people teaching how to create a course or group program. The pitch is that an income ceiling is inevitable with a service business, so you need to diversify your income streams.

The premise here is inherently flawed, as it positions the shift from a service business (one-to-one model) to courses/programs (a one-to-many model) as natural and normal.

Unfortunately, the shift from services to a course, program, or product business is much more complicated than it appears. For the one-to-many model to be viable, you need to build a solid (and sometimes sizable) audience. Plus, creating, selling, and running courses, programs, and products all require a very different set of skills.

So the real question we need to explore is if there's really an income ceiling for service business owners.

The truth? The answer is complicated, and that's what we're going to dive into now, along with specific strategy options to help you avoid hitting an income ceiling.

THE INCOME CEILING: A REALITY CHECK

One of the reasons I started doing the work I do with solo service business owners is the result of being able to figure out something that many of my business friends and peers didn't. Trust me when I say I didn't set out to be a consultant who works with service business owners, so it's a happy accident that I'm here today.

In 2014 and 2015, I was a solo business owner and made significant shifts in my business that led to revenue growth. After years of relatively flat revenue (and income), I finally figured it out. People started to notice and asked me what I was doing, and I moved into doing more business-type consulting.

I'm going to share some of the specific strategies I've used to break income ceilings (and that I share with my clients), but it's important that you have the context for why you will bump up against an income ceiling at some point.

It's also important to note that every business, and business owner, is unique. Where an income ceiling may happen for you will vary wildly, and can't be fully separated from your values and personal goals.

As discussed in Chapter 4, salary is intensely personal. Before we start looking at strategies to grow through common income ceilings, I want to remind you that we're not trying to grow a giant business and make buckets of money here. Remember, we're talking about Staying Solo®, and the real objective is to ensure you're meeting your goals and not engaging in harmful business practices.

Ultimately, there are multiple factors that contribute to a potential income ceiling, from experience, skills, pricing, and delivery, to packages, clientele, industry, and more. We'll address each of these when we look at potential solutions.

THE STRATEGY STACK

Strategy is a word that's thrown around in business conversations, but what does it actually mean, particularly in the context of Staying Solo? By definition strategy is about having a set of plans to get you to a specific goal. Yet so many business owners confuse strategy with tactics, or simply go into action mode without understanding how those actions impact other aspects of the business.

That combined with the fact that to have a truly sustainable service business in place you need a solid foundation, is what led me to create something I call the Strategy Stack.

It's loosely based on the concept of the four Ps (product, place, promotion, and price) conceptualized in 1960 by E. Jerome McCarthy, which is a widely accepted framework for marketing strategy.

The Strategy Stack is designed to illustrate the options available to you as a solopreneur to break the income ceiling as you build your business, while reinforcing the fact that if you don't have the fundamentals nailed down (namely people and position) the rest of your strategy options likely won't work.

Over the next few chapters we'll explore all of the elements of the Strategy Stack, followed by an entire chapter on the one thing every solo service business can do to make more money.

PEOPLE: WHO ARE YOU REALLY SELLING TO?

While your business model is already determined as a service business owner, the next most strategic (and honestly crucial) decisions you make are related to your people.

Typically when solopreneurs are struggling to market or sell their services, they look for ways to adjust pricing or reformulate their packages, overlooking the reality that they don't have a solid foundation when it comes to their people.

When I refer to people, I'm really talking about two key things that will determine your success or failure: what industry you work in and who your target client is.

Industry

I won't sugarcoat it. What industry you work in will absolutely impact when you hit an income ceiling. Different industries have different thresholds for how much they'll pay for services.

This is why my business went from working with entrepreneurs, to locally-based small businesses, to tech and professional services firms. It was an evolution.

First, I found that the entrepreneur market had five-star expectations but a tiny budget. For local small businesses, the ones we worked with had money to invest but required an extreme amount of handholding, which cut into profits. For the type of work we do, tech clients are ideal as they have the budgets and how they work is aligned with how we want to work.

If you find that you're constantly hitting the high end of pricing in your market alongside other constraints, it may be time to explore a new industry. Remember, there may be markets adjacent to the one you already work in, or have past experience in, that would be a fairly easy shift for your business.

Target Client

In the case of your target client, you need a clearly defined one that you know forward and backward. I know that sounds obvious, but one of the biggest mistakes I see service business owners make is focusing on the *wrong* audience.

For example, if you're selling copywriting services to B2B clients, you need to understand their need for the service and pain points, who makes the buying decisions, how they do their research, and what they're looking for. These insights will enable you to target the right person with the right messaging and marketing.

As content marketer Lee Densmer tells her clients, "find the person with the problem you solve who ALSO has access to the decision making power and budget."

Looking at our example, if the person who makes the buying decision is a VP of marketing, you need to market in a way that targets them, and not someone at a more junior level with little influence in these decisions.

While you may be able to make some sales in this situation, by being more specific you'll be able to get high-quality and potentially more clients.

The other potential pitfall with your target client is having an audience that's too broad. The more general your potential client pool is, the harder it is to speak to their unique challenges and capture their attention.

Broad categories of people such as "moms" or "women entrepreneurs" simply aren't a target client; you need to take the time and energy to be unequivocal about who your ideal clients really are. Instead of "women entrepreneurs," go deeper into their demographics, psychographics, problems, beliefs, and values.

If that seems intimidating, I hear you. Many times we hesitate to get ultra specific as we don't want to turn away potential clients, when that's exactly what we need to do to simplify our sales and marketing while growing our client roster.

POSITIONING: WHAT SETS YOU APART?

Why should a client choose to work with you? It should be an easy question, but I know for most of us, it's not!

Most service business owners are much more comfortable being behind the scenes, so clearly articulating *why* a client should work with us can be a challenge.

This is your positioning which enables you to articulate your value with clarity and authority.

I'm not saying that you suddenly need to have slick sales skills, but rather that you need to be able to tell people why you're the right choice. Otherwise you may end up struggling, especially if you're working in a saturated or highly competitive market.

It's really easy to decide that as you're a solopreneur you don't need to focus on positioning. That's a mistake in the long run as you may blend into the crowd, end up with poor-fit clients, or make less money.

Think about the brands you love and are loyal to. It's always about so much more than the product. Maybe it's how it makes you feel, or the problem it solves for you.

That's what the right positioning can do for you as it helps build trust, loyalty, and connection with your potential clients.

Honestly, this is an area most service business owners grossly underestimate when it's the backbone of any successful business. Without solid positioning, it's that much harder to market and sell your services, which is why this is at the base of the Strategy Stack.

Here are a few questions to help you explore your positioning:

- What skills and experience do you bring?
- What past client successes can you share?

- What's different about your approach?
- What problem do you solve?
- What do clients need to know about working with you?
- What results can your clients expect?

If you're tempted to avoid this, I'm going to encourage you to focus on this even more, because there's nothing more powerful than having clarity and confidence about your value to clients.

PACKAGING: WHAT ARE YOU SELLING?

The next strategy you need to nail down in your business relates to your packages. While these get talked about a lot for service business owners, as you become more experienced, you may need to find new ways to present them.

Before we dive into different options for packaging your services, let's briefly look at what to consider as you design your service. It's easy to see a trendy way of offering services and think it's right for you as it's being hyped up. In reality, we need to slow down and think about what will work best for everyone involved.

What Works Best for You?

Before you decide anything, start by figuring out how you'll best work. Do you like short sprints, or long-term relationships? Do you work well under pressure, or do you need more processing time?

Don't fall into the trap of picking a service that *seems* easy without assessing if it's aligned with how you like to work. You'll want to show up at your absolute best.

What Works Best for Clients?

Next up, when you offer services, you need to consider what will best serve the client. It's hard to sell a service, let alone get results, if you can't get potential clients to buy into how it works.

Assess how the service can be set up to get the best possible result for the client. Sometimes the best result will come from speed; other times from going slow. It may be working intensely, or following a longer, more structured process.

There isn't a right or wrong answer, but it's so easy to design a service based on what we want, while forgetting about what will deliver the desired result for the client.

What are the Marketing and Sales Requirements?

Finally, you'll want to dig into what's required for marketing and selling each type of service — that may help you quickly decide what the best option is.

If you do more short-term projects, you'll likely need to do more marketing to have a steady flow of clients. If you do longer-term retainer engagements, you'll likely need to do less marketing overall.

Again, there's no right or wrong, but this is a critical consideration that's easily overlooked by so many service providers. Designing your dream service is one thing, but you need to be ready to market and sell it with confidence in order for it to work.

Your Target Market: Coaching and Consulting vs Done-for-You Services

What type of service business you run will absolutely impact what packaging approach is best for you. There are some big differences between coaching businesses and those that offer done-for-you services.

With coaching and consulting the deliverable is time with the provider, and during that time together you'll get value through your interactions with them. With done-for-you work, you're typically doing deliverable work, so what you're selling is different.

How you sell coaching versus done-for-you services is also quite different. A coach or consultant will often sell a package directly from a sales page, while a service provider will often need to send a proposal. A coach may jump on a discovery call or offer free coaching, while someone offering deliverables may want to screen people more carefully to ensure they actually want to work together.

The final difference between these two types of services is around pricing. Setting prices for coaching and consulting can be relatively simple, while there's more nuance and complexity around done-for-you services. With done-for-you services, you're creating deliverables for the client which makes it harder to predict how much time or energy may be involved.

THE OVERLOOKED PART OF PACKAGING: DELIVERY STRATEGY

When I refer to a delivery strategy, I mean "how" you deliver your services. This may be projects, retainers, intensives, or even pricing by the hour. This is often overlooked when people create packages, and needs more consideration as you grow.

Usually, when we start our businesses, we gravitate naturally toward one of these delivery strategies, and our inclination is to stick with it as we know it works for us. If you're bumping up against an income ceiling, it's likely time to consider adding a new delivery model into the mix.

Why? It comes down to the needs of different types of clients and how they may work with you. For example, if you only offer retainers, you're missing out on opportunities to serve additional clients who may want a one-time or short-term engagement. In this case, you may want to add a shorter, more contained service that enables you to work with a whole new set of clients and generate more revenue.

Here's a rundown on the most common delivery models for solo service business owners, including what they are and the benefits of each one. I'm also going to share some examples and my own experiences to help put a real-world spin on this.

Billing by the Hour

This is definitely one of the most common, but most maligned options out there. I get it, hourly billing can be tricky and it's often viewed as transactional.

What often gets missed in the conversation about hourly billing is how simple it can be to sell (especially if you're just starting out), as people understand the concept of paying for hours.

Technically, with this type of offer you're trading time for dollars. However, I want to be clear here. If we're working, we're *always* trading our time and talents for money. That's how the system works.

Pros: You can have stronger boundaries around the scope of work as it's capped by hours or budget. In my experience, this has usually made the scope creep conversation go better with clients.
Cons: Some clients have no concept of how long things really take and may view you as padding your hours. It's always a possibility, but I'd also argue this type of client will push the limit of any arrangement that's in place.

Hourly Packages or Blocks of Hours

Hourly packages are a way to make hourly billing easier to manage and to ensure you get paid upfront for the hours you're going to work.

That way there's a clear understanding of what's to be done and how many hours it will take.

With hourly packages, you can bill these monthly, quarterly, or in whatever increment works best for you. I highly recommend that you do have an expiry on hours blocks, and that they're pre-paid and non-refundable.

Pros: Sets a boundary with the client about how many hours are involved, and enables you to manage scope of work that's not clearly defined. It ensures that you can set boundaries around minimums, as no one wants to bill for only 30 minutes.

Cons: Clients can have unrealistic expectations about how quickly work can be done. There's a need to track hours and keep the client in the loop.

Flat Rate Projects

If you work in a world with set deliverables, flat rate packages or projects are probably a great fit for you. You're able to charge a specific price based on defined outputs and your specific process.

In many ways, this type of package is my favorite as it's easy to manage and execute. Where flat rate packages can bite you is if you're in a situation where scope creep is possible and you don't have clear boundaries. With this, you need to include a set number of opportunities for client feedback and carefully manage the entire process so the client isn't taking up far more time than expected.

For many of my clients that offer coaching, this type of offer works great for them. They'll have a package with a set number of calls, as well as additional support and resources.

Pros: Great for projects with a set amount of predictable deliverables, because you're not penalized for efficiency as with an hourly rate.

Cons: Potential for scope creep and you'll need clear boundaries around work that's outside of what's included.

Retainers

You've probably heard the term *retainer* used in different ways, so I want to explain briefly what a retainer is.

There are two specific approaches to retainers.

The first is where someone pays you a set amount in order to "retain" your services and then you bill against that. This is a common model used by lawyers and professional service providers. For example, the client pays you $1,500 a month, and you bill at $150 dollars per hour. Each time you do work for them you deduct the amount from the total retainer.

The other approach is having ongoing commitments (usually weekly or monthly) to work with clients. This may be either for a specific number of hours or a predefined set of deliverables.

If you're wondering what you could offer on a retainer basis:

- **For coaching**, you could have a six-month coaching agreement that's essentially a retainer with your client with set calls or access to you.
- **For consulting**, you may have an agreement to be available X hours per month on an as-needed basis.
- **For creatives,** you can have a retainer with set deliverables or hours available for assignments in a month.

Pros: Ensures continuity month after month. Plus, it helps reduce the need to focus as much on lead gen and there are many process efficiencies gained by working with clients longer-term.

Cons: Retainers can be repetitive and boring for some people.

Consulting Engagements

Consulting engagements are often overlooked by service providers, but they're definitely worth considering. Over the years I've done a number of these types of engagements and they've been very lucrative.

This type of offer works really well when you have clients who value strategy and will pay for someone to come in and tell them what to do. It sounds overly simplistic, but you're literally being paid for your expertise and to "consult" on their needs.

This could be done for everything from team management to brand strategy to specific tools. Think of it as being the special guest star who gets paid to come in and boost ratings on a TV show.

This type of consulting can be done for all types of businesses and structured as a short-term engagement where you dig into something specific and then provide your recommendations.

Pros: It's a limited-time engagement, where you're hired for your expertise. You can charge premium pricing and there's a clear path to ongoing work.

Cons: You need to deliver quickly. Consults may require more relationship building or marketing than you currently do for your services.

Day Rates/VIP Days

Day rates or VIP days are a classic consulting approach used by many types of organizations.

It's something I often did for clients in my agency days, and when I was freelancing. They'd literally buy my day for a specific project or event so that would have my full focus.

As an offer, an intensive or day-bound gig can be very alluring, but it's important to ensure that it will work best for you and the client. This can be a very intense way to work, and you need to know that you can show up and perform.

Pros: These are short-term engagements, where clients pay a premium for speed. There is no ongoing client commitment.
Cons: There's a constant need to market and find new clients, plus pressure to deliver quickly. It can be energy-intensive on the days you're booked.

Deciding on Your Delivery Model

- Is this delivery model aligned with how I want to work?
- Will this work for my target clients?
- Will this model work for the amount of marketing I want to do or not do?
- How will I manage my energy with this delivery model?
- Does the timeline for this delivery model work for the type of work I do?
- Do I want short-term commitments or longer-term engagements? Or a mixture of both?
- How will I avoid scope creep?
- How will I manage client expectations?

PACKAGING STRATEGY: KEY DECISIONS

Now, let's get into your packaging strategy, which is about what you do (and don't) deliver. This may seem tactical, however, it's a strategy as your packages should be much more than a list of deliverables with a price attached.

If you find you have potential clients but you don't close as many as you'd like, take some time to examine your packages and get curious.

Consider: Are you solving a specific problem and communicating the result you deliver? Or are you providing a laundry list of tasks you'll do for them?

The more you can dial that in, the more clients you can close. Plus, you'll be able to charge more as you're solving a stated, real problem for clients, making you a must-have rather than a nice-to-have.

That's exactly how having the right packages helps you earn more and bust through your income ceiling.

Simplify Everything with Packages

Whenever I go out to eat, I'm pretty excited about all of the possibilities for what I could have. But if it's somewhere we've been before, about 80% of the time, I end up getting the same one or two dishes.

Why? Because I'm overwhelmed by all the options, I go with what I know will work for me.

This is how potential clients feel when it comes to figuring out how they could work with us. Even if you offer a wide variety of services, saying "I can do all the things" while not being able to clearly articulate those things makes it stressful for your potential client.

This is why you need to strategically package your services.

The reality is that not all packages are created equal. Usually when people start out creating packages, they just take what they're doing, give it a name, and sell it.

That's a great place to start, but for you to stay solo, and not have your income flatline, you need packages that are closely aligned with your client's most specific and urgent needs.

Use the following questions to create packages from a place of intention, or to revamp the ones you already have.

1. What do you currently offer that you want to charge more for?

When you're looking to create a package, the best place to start is with what you're already doing and want to charge more for. The idea of the package isn't for you to start randomly offering a bunch of things, but rather for you to do more of what you want to be doing and get paid in a way that helps you reach your business goals.

For example, if you offer a copywriting service that you know your clients love, but you need it to be more profitable and efficient, you can revisit the positioning and packaging of the offer to ensure it's working for you. In this case, you may decide to remove aspects of the package to streamline it, improve how you communicate it, and adjust the pricing.

2. What service(s) do you offer that you can systematize?

Over the years, I've created a number of packages, and the easiest ones to sell — and deliver — were highly systematized. Even if custom work is involved, there should be a well-defined system for your services that you follow each and every time you work with a client.

The key is being able to productize what you're doing so that it's repeatable. The more you can reap the benefits of repetition, the more profitable your packages will be.

For example, if you're a designer and you often create logos for clients, instead of quoting each client based on the project, you create a package. This includes a specific process that you follow for each client which helps position you as an expert and save time as you're not constantly figuring out the basics of each project.

3. Who is this service for?

Before you can sell your package, you need to ensure that there's a market for what you're offering and that you know who you're selling it to.

Take the time — before you get too excited about your package — to define who the ideal client is for you to work with. Be as specific as possible, and ensure it's something that people really and truly need.

If you're not clear who the package is really for, time to go back to the drawing board and do some market research.

4. What makes you the perfect person to hire for this specific service?

People hire people they trust, which means they're looking to hire someone who can do what they say they can do. Spend some time getting clear on why they should hire you and what unique skills or experiences you bring to the table.

Don't be modest; this is an opportunity for you to really own your awesomeness, and share why you're so good at what you do. It may feel awkward, but trust me, people want to know. If you're holding back, you're just making it harder to market and sell your packages.

If you're not sure, ask your most recent clients what their experience was like working with you, and what results they were able to achieve.

5. How will you deliver the service to the client?

You can have the best idea in the world for a package — and there can be a real need for it — but if it's going to be a real pain in the butt to deliver to the client, it's likely not worth it.

Let's say you design a package that requires four phone calls, and you loathe being on the phone. This is not going to be a winning package for you.

6. What benefits will the client experience when you're done working together?

When a client hires you, they're looking for the transformation that will occur as a result of working together. They don't want to hear about how they get a beautiful workbook, but rather what the end result of your work together will be and how that makes their business or life better.

Digging into the results your clients get and being able to share those in a way that paints a picture for your prospective clients is key. Also, this is where case studies, testimonials, or examples for your package can help act as proof of what you can really do.

In the free Staying Solo Starter Kit you'll get access to Purposeful Packages, a workshop to help you with packaging your services. It includes a workbook and video to walk you through the key decisions to make about your packages. You can get access at: www.stayingsolokit.com.

PROMOTION: MAKING IT EFFECTIVE AND EFFICIENT

Staying Solo® isn't a book about marketing, but you know that you need a way to consistently bring in new clients.

Typically, referrals are the number one way that the solo business owners I work with get clients, which is entirely normal. However, as your business grows and you find yourself wanting to make more money without needing to work more, your promotion strategy becomes essential.

Promotion isn't about having a steady stream of leads, but the RIGHT leads who value your services and are willing to pay your prices. You don't need to be everywhere or do everything to promote your offers, but you do need a plan that enables you to get the number of leads you need to reach your goals.

In chapter 8, I shared a number of marketing systems so I don't need to get into those specific tactics. Instead, let's discuss what you need to consider so your promotion is strategic and not wasting precious time.

As someone opting to stay solo, you have limited time and resources, which means you want your marketing to count. The key is finding the sweet spot between marketing you can actually execute (and sustain) while getting you in front of your potential clients.

Instead of chasing trends and jumping on the latest social media platform get clear on the following about your target client:

- Where do they look for information related to your services?
- What type of information are they looking for?
- What formats do they prefer?

- What triggers them to consider these solutions?
- What events or platforms do they trust?
- What influences their buying decisions?

You may not have answers to every single one of these questions, but the more you understand about your clients, the easier it is for you to make strategic decisions about your marketing and promotion.

Over the years clients have often asked me which marketing tactic is the "best" one for them to use, and that requires a nuanced answer.

The best marketing activities are the ones that will actually get you results and — most importantly — the ones you'll stick with. While certain strategies might technically be more effective for reaching your target client, the real magic happens when you choose approaches that feel natural and require the least amount of effort on your part. If it's something you're good at and enjoy doing, you're far more likely to stay consistent — and that's what leads to real results over time.

WHAT STRATEGIES WILL YOU IMPLEMENT?

If you're currently facing an income ceiling (or are quickly on your way towards one), now's the time to revisit your Strategy Stack. Remember, what got you *here* won't automatically get you *there*, and being intentional about how you serve your clients enables you to simplify your services, and make more money.

You may notice that I skipped one of the Ps in the Strategy Stack, pricing — we'll tackle this in detail in the next chapter.

Chapter 10

Your Pricing Strategy

Pricing is one of the most critical yet complex parts of being a service business owner. It impacts everything from the types of clients you work with to how much money you can pay yourself, and even how you feel about your work.

As a seasoned service business owner, I know all too well what a rollercoaster it can be to price your services. In working with service business owners, pricing is one of the areas in which they need the most input and support.

Listen, I'm not going to knock pricing strategy as a proven way to boost your revenue and break the income ceiling. It absolutely works. It's worked for me, and I've seen it work countless times for my clients.

But pricing strategy is just that: a *strategy*. It's not these arbitrary "just raise your prices" or "charge your worth" BS statements that we're swimming in all day long in the online business world.

For you to raise your prices, you absolutely need to ensure that:

- There's a proven need for what you have to offer.
- That you can clearly articulate the value and results you deliver.
- Your position in the market and target audience.

That's why this is the last strategy I'm sharing with you in *Staying Solo*, as all of the other strategic elements discussed until now create a compound effect. Those small, smart, and strategic decisions add up to you being able to raise your prices in a way that's realistic, trustworthy, and sustainable.

If you're hesitating about just the idea of raising your prices, I want you to consider what happens if you don't ever raise your prices. You won't just be dealing with an income ceiling; you'll be struggling to keep up with the ever-increasing cost of living.

If you had a regular 9 to 5 job, you would likely (at least I hope) get a raise as your skills and experience increased. Your value as a service provider increases over time, and the reality is that market rates also climb over time.

Never raising your prices is simply not sustainable.

There's nothing wrong with raising your prices, as long as you do it in a way that's thoughtful and intentional. Take time to look at your current pricing and where you may have room to raise prices.

Here's a pro tip: if you have more client work than you can handle, or nearly everyone says yes to working with you, you have pricing capacity and can raise your prices.

Finally, no conversation about pricing would be complete without acknowledging that the economy goes through periodic cycles, and you may need to adjust based on those bigger forces.

If you're not feeling comfortable raising your prices right now, this is just one strategy. You can use it at the right moment for you and your clients.

THE PSYCHOLOGY OF PRICING, TRUST, AND YOUR CLIENTS

You can set your prices however you like, but if your clients won't pay that price, you'll struggle more than necessary. You need to understand what's happening for your clients and factor that into your pricing decisions.

Typically, when we talk about the psychology of pricing in the online business world, we focus on scammy shortcuts to manipulate your clients. I don't want to talk about charm, or high ticket pricing, or anything of that nature. Instead, let's explore how your potential clients may perceive your pricing.

Research from Deloitte shows that consumers are anxious about rising prices. About 75% of consumers are "concerned about rising prices for everyday purchases." I'm sure that's unsurprising to anyone reading this book, as we all feel the impacts of inflation daily.

Overall, consumers are under strain and are concerned about their financial health, including their savings and level of debt.

Our businesses operate against this backdrop, and the Deloitte report found that "consumer sentiment around inflation goes beyond mere concern." As prices rise, there's a perception that "companies themselves are also at fault." This leads to "a clear lack of trust brewing," and this "unfair pricing sentiment is correlated with weaker spending intentions."

In short, especially in times of high inflation, your potential clients are likely weary of rising prices, meaning you need to focus on building trust like never before.

Research from PwC referred to trust as "a currency, altering loyalty and buying decisions for customers." In the survey they conducted, "91% of customers say they would buy from a company that gained their trust. Of that group, only 14% say they would buy significantly more. On the other hand, of the 71% of customers who say they would buy less if a company lost their trust, a whopping 73% say they would spend significantly less."

While this is primarily consumer research related to large companies, it's incredibly relevant to all buying decisions in an uncertain economy. Your potential clients are looking to you to provide context for your pricing so they understand the value you deliver and don't feel like you're unfairly profiting.

Remember that when it comes to the pricing of services, your clients may have wildly different ideas of how much your services could cost. Research from Anderson and Simester indicates that many consumers have poor price knowledge, so they rely on pricing cues.

Pricing cues such as sale signs, prices ending in 9, and pricing guarantees, guide buying decisions. For service businesses, these practices aren't particularly helpful. Still, you can provide pricing cues to your customers by ensuring they have insight into the offer and a general idea of pricing.

Think about it from your potential client's perspective: Who will they trust more if they don't have a good handle on the pricing? The person with no pricing and very little detail, or the person with a straightforward process and a stated "starts at" price?

Transparency is a compelling signpost that leads to trust from your potential clients and needs to be a foundational part of pricing considerations.

EVALUATING YOUR CURRENT PRICING

Before you develop a pricing strategy you need to check on your current pricing.

To evaluate your pricing, here are a few key questions to explore:

- How much do you currently charge for each of your services?
- Are you making sales of your services at that price? What's your close rate with potential clients for each service?
- What services do you sell the most? The least?
- How much does each service cost you to deliver? (Be sure to include any hard costs.)
- Are there any hidden costs you're not accounting for in your pricing?

There's zero point in considering raising your prices if you don't have a good handle on the basics. Your pricing needs to be realistic but not leave you short.

Too often, pricing results from guesswork, not actual costs or time involved. This quickly leads to undercharging, overworking, and an inability to pay yourself a professional salary.

Next, we need to do the math:

- What's your average hourly rate? (Even if you don't charge by the hour.)
- What does your hourly rate need to be?
- How many "billable hours" do you work in a week?
- How much time do you spend delivering a service?

These numbers give you baseline data to work with as you determine your ideal pricing.

ALIGN YOUR PRICING WITH YOUR GOALS

We all have specific goals in our business, including how much we want to pay ourselves and how much we want to work.

If you're unsure how much you want to pay yourself, check out the Personal Salary Goal Calculator in the Staying Solo Starter Kit that goes with this book at www.stayingsolokit.com.

And if you're thinking you can keep working at the pace you're currently working, I want you to sit with that for a moment. Is that realistic?

Use these questions to explore what would best serve you:

- What if you work with fewer clients at a higher price?
- What if you work with 10% more clients and raise your prices by 10%?
- What if you work with 20% more clients and charge 20% more?
- How much less do you need to work?

Again, play with the scenarios. See how small changes to each variable impact your ability to reach your goals and have a life. Look at your number of clients, how much you work, and how much you want to work.

For example, if you made $70k this year and worked with ten clients to reach that number but want to get to $85k next year, you need to increase revenue by 21.4%.

To achieve that number, you could increase prices:

- By 25% across the board and work with fewer clients
- By 15% and take on one more client
- By 10% and take on two more clients

This is why your pricing needs to be intentional, as you have options. However, you also need to consider how your potential price increases impact you *and* your clients. If you can't sell your service at the new price, or your prospective clients feel like you're overcharging, you're setting yourself up to struggle.

Remember, the goal is always to strike a balance so you're serving both yourself and your clients. You need to be compensated like the professional you are, but in a way aligned with the market you serve.

THE ART OF RAISING YOUR PRICES

The math is one thing, but then there's the delicate art of implementing price rises. For many, this will feel very uncomfortable and may lead to you avoiding it, but trust me when I say that is a very unsustainable business move.

Assuming you've gone through the process of determining your pricing strategy, the next step is to raise those prices. I don't mean that in a cavalier, celebrity-entrepreneur-type way, but rather that you actually have to follow through.

I always recommend an incremental price increase with adequate notice for your existing clients so they have time to plan accordingly. Give them at least 30 days' notice, but ideally 60 days', when raising your prices.

Also, pick your moment strategically. This is a conversation for when your current clients are delighted, not when they're stressed out or the relationship is rocky. Happy clients are happy to pay increased prices, while unhappy ones will likely question if it's worth it.

For new clients, they'll get your new price. Put that price on your website and your proposals, and use it consistently. Once you book a handful of clients at that price, you'll be confident to raise the price again until you reach your target price.

THE MENTAL JUNK OF PRICING YOUR SERVICES

When you're working on pricing your services, you may find a lot of mental junk comes up for you. You may be thinking:

- Who am I to charge this?
- Am I really worth this?
- Will anyone pay this price?
- Is this price too greedy?
- What will people think of me?

First, I want to affirm that it's entirely normal if these thoughts are coming up. I've been pricing services my entire career, and I still question if my pricing is totally out to lunch at times.

Dr. Brad Klontz has pioneered the field of financial psychology with his work around *money scripts*, which are our beliefs around money. These scripts, which are shaped by the stories we have about money, impact how we think, feel, and behave around money.

While money mindset is a frequent topic of discussion among business coaches and online business teachers, I've personally found the money scripts more helpful for both me and my clients — they provide more insight into what we're thinking and how the scripts impact money-related decisions in our pricing.

My primary money script is what Klontz calls *money focus*, where my solution is to have more money, which means I'm prone to overwork. Knowing this has helped me ensure that I'm pricing my services in a way that means I'm not obsessing over making more money.

Funnily, my lowest scoring money script is *money status*, which equates net worth with self-worth. Maybe that explains why I don't find luxury lifestyle marketing appealing?

This insight into how your brain works when it comes to money is critical to your pricing strategy. Case in point: my clients with a dominant *money avoidance* script would like to never raise their prices or even talk about pricing.

No matter what you may think or feel about money, it's a necessary part of running your business. Plus, pricing is one of the most powerful and strategic levers you have.

I've never ever regretted raising my prices. Not once. And most of the time, I wish I'd done it sooner.

The same goes for my clients. No one has ever told me they wish they'd not raised their prices. That's likely because the majority of service business owners are not charging nearly enough.

COMMON PRICING TRAPS

If you're hesitant to raise your prices, I want to share a few common traps that service businesses fall into.

Prices That Are Too Low

When you're first starting out, it's easy to fall into the trap of pricing things too low.

I'm a big fan of pricing things so you're able to get feedback and nail down the model of what you're doing, but still get paid fairly. That allows you to get feedback and refine your processes while gaining more and more experience.

What you shouldn't do is offer bargain pricing as it causes a number of issues. First of all, you're more likely to be resentful about the work you're doing as you're not being fairly compensated.

Then there's the fact that your pricing tells a story. If you're constantly pricing yourself at the low end of the market, you're sending a message that you're not all that awesome at what you do.

Your low price doesn't convey confidence that you can deliver results, and perfect-for-you clients may very well be turned off by it. (This is a red flag for me when I'm hiring contractors as I worry they won't be confident enough to step up and deliver what we need.)

On the other hand, low prices often attract the wrong type of clients as they are selecting you not for what you can do for them but for the price. Working with clients like this means you won't receive the kind of feedback you need to reach clients who will value the higher-priced service.

Prices That Are Too High

You've probably heard the whole "charge what you're worth" pricing advice. Quite frankly, it's crap. It's often used as a way to justify prices that are inflated or completely bananas.

The truth is: it's impossible to charge what you're worth. Who decides what you're worth? How do you quantify that?

Exactly. You're priceless. It's impossible to put a number on human worth.

So, how do you know if your pricing is too high?

If you consistently can't book clients at that rate or you have a lot of conversations with would-be clients that say no based on the price, that's a sign that your price is too high or that you're doing a poor job of communicating the real value of what you offer.

At that point, you've got a choice. You either find a way to stand out so you can charge a premium price, or you understand that you're a commodity and need to price as such.

It's simple economics. If you're a me-too in a sea of people offering the exact same thing, very few people are going to pay top dollar as they know there's an ample "supply" of people who can do the job as well as you can.

It's only when you can stand out, own your authority, and tap into a real need that only you can fill that you're able to command top-shelf prices for your services.

Again, your price tells a story, so you need to think about where you want to sit in the market. Ideally, if you want to charge prices at the high end of the spectrum, you need to find a way to position yourself as a "category of one" so there's no question as to why that price is what it is.

Finding the Pricing Sweet Spot

Finding the sweet spot for your pricing comes down to being willing to experiment and shift over time.

Each time I introduce a new service, I use an intro price to test things out and to get experience with that service. Then, I strategically move the price up over time as there's more and more demand for that service. That strategy has enabled me to charge premium prices where they are warranted and to find the right price point for each offering.

As you consider your pricing, it really comes down to three core things:

- Need for what you have to offer.
- Perception of you and what you're offering.
- The value of your service and the results you deliver.

The key to pricing your services comes down to having the confidence to be honest about each of these items and for you to work with your pricing in a way that gets you paid and helps you grow.

Your pricing of services is a critical part of your overall business success, but bad advice is everywhere. It can get in our heads and hold us back, especially in an uncertain economic climate where buying decisions are more complex.

Focus on doing good work, providing excellent service, and delivering real value to your clients, while ensuring potential clients trust you and understand your offer and pricing. Those things alone can and will go a long way to helping you price your services in a way that works for everyone

THE TRUE POWER OF PRICING

Ontraport expert Alejandra Ortega had the goal of increasing her monthly revenue when I first started working with her. But there was a catch. She didn't want to work more and was committed to working an average of 20 hours a week with ample time off.

Over the past few years she has steadily raised her prices for new clients, boosting her revenue to a point where she's making a healthy full-time salary working part-time hours.

This wasn't a quick process, or one that I can promise will happen for everyone, but with a commitment to diligently raising her prices and ensuring a high level of client experience, Alejandra is an example of what's possible for solo service business owners.

If you'd like more pricing resources, you'll find two pricing calculators in the resources for this book which you can grab as part of the Staying Solo Starter Kit at www.stayingsolokit.com.

In the next chapter, I'm going to share my preferred way to break through an income ceiling. It's a way that worked for me and for many of my clients: selling strategy.

Chapter 11

Selling Strategy

While you might have needed a helping hand with strategy in your own business, I'm willing to bet that you can take one look at a client's business and know exactly what strategy they need in terms of what you do.

You know what else I'm willing to bet? That you're giving this valuable knowledge away for free.

There's one thing I want you to walk away from this chapter knowing how to do and that's being able to sell your ability to strategize for your clients. Take some time and consider where you're leaking your strategy knowledge and then figure out a way to ensure you can charge for it.

In my own experience, all of the things I've discussed so far contributed to me being able to break through an income ceiling. But hands down, the biggest difference was focusing on ways to sell strategy or provide strategizing services.

I have developed the Sell the Strategy® method, which builds on the packaging strategy I shared above and takes it to the next level. If you're already successfully selling packages, you likely have a hidden strategy in them.

Say you're a book editor who works with clients who self-publish, but every client asks dozens of questions about the publishing process. That's strategy you're giving away for free.

Or maybe you're a content writer who needs to understand your client's audience to do your job, but you handhold them through the process of how to nail that down. Again, strategy for free.

You might be a speaker coach who can give fantastic feedback on delivery, but you spend more time reworking clients' content and messaging because the gigs they're getting aren't a great fit. Yep, free strategy.

See how you might end up resenting this part of your work?

If you do retainer work, selling strategy can be offered as a project for a different audience. If you do projects, it can be the compulsory first step in working together. And if you work with day rates, you could be doing a strategy package in your intensives.

Selling strategy is about so much more than being able to get paid for work you're doing, or commanding more for the work you do. For me, and so many of my clients, it helped them see themselves as a true expert, while positioning them in that way for their clients.

When you're selling strategy, you show up differently with clients as you're clear and confident. That impacts every aspect of your business in a positive way.

SELL THE STRATEGY®: STEPPING UP YOUR SERVICE BUSINESS

As service providers, there are definitely situations where we can feel underpaid and unappreciated, which leads to frustration and resentment. I mean, who's not felt frustrated by a client or like they were on the verge of burnout? These are very real situations that we face. I know I've definitely been there, but they're in no way inevitable.

While I'm not one for sweeping solutions, I believe the gamechanger for me and my business has the potential to help service business owners be paid like the experts they are, and create a different dynamic within their business.

In recent years, I noticed a pattern where this came up time and time again with my clients. In the half-day intensives, we'd end up focusing on this strategy work in nearly every session. With members of my masterminds, we'd devote attention to this in our one-on-one calls.

Honestly, this is one of those things I thought that everyone knew to do in their service business, but I looked at this pattern and realized that wasn't the case.

After doing some research and talking to my clients, I recognized that this was far beyond a signature service and needed its own name for the process.

This brings us to Sell the Strategy® and how it can help you in your business.

What Is Sell the Strategy®?

Back in 2014, I was at a crossroads. I'd shifted to focus on working more with online businesses, and I was struggling.

I had clients, I was meeting my goals, but I was grappling with feeling undervalued, even disrespected at times.

I was busting my ass writing proposals and giving away strategies for free. I can't even tell you how many times potential clients walked away with thousands of dollars of free work that they were able to put into action.

Another challenge was that I had great relationships with my clients, but I was the doer. Every time they'd bring in an outside consultant to do the strategy part, I'd die a little inside. I was watching them pay other people when they could have been paying me.

Then there was the entire hot mess of working with clients who didn't value strategy. There's nothing wrong with tactical execution, but doing it without a strategy is a freaking nightmare. It felt transactional. Plus, the end result would typically suffer.

After a series of frustrating and demoralizing situations which I'll spare you the details of, I decided something had to change. I looked at how, in my past roles working with agencies, we'd approach new client engagements. There was one thing that kept occurring to me — everything started with a strategy. It wasn't given away for free, even when we were pitching to huge multinationals. The strategy was a prerequisite to our work together and it often took a considerable upfront commitment.

Total lightbulb moment.

So I started offering strategy as the first step in any work I do, and I'm not even exaggerating a little bit when I say it changed *everything*.

WHY STRATEGY?

Separating out and getting paid to work on the strategy piece helped shift so many things for me and my business. One of the biggest ones was that the quality of my clients improved as I was only working with people who took a strategic approach.

It quickly became a filter for who was and wasn't a good fit for my business.

When I started using this approach with my copywriting and content clients by selling content strategy first and making it a requirement of working with me, I screened out people who just wanted some "quick and easy" web copy.

Another thing happened in that process. Before I required clients to pay for content strategy, I would find myself doing it anyway. I was doing it for free as a way to ensure the content or copy being written was meeting their business goals.

Getting paid for strategy meant I wasn't doing it for free anymore. If they weren't willing to pay, we weren't going to work together.

Plus, not giving away strategy for free in the proposal process? Speeds up everything and creates a firm boundary from day one.

Over time, I noticed I have not just better quality clients, but stronger client relationships. Instead of having clients overlook my counsel in favor of shiny objects or "it" copywriters, I was seen and treated as the expert I am.

My input and strategic thinking were trusted and respected. No more bringing in flashy experts and me feeling disgruntled.

Another big benefit of putting strategy first is that my clients got better results. I've experienced this. It's not surprising really, but my requirement to do strategy first ultimately meant no more random acts of marketing that didn't add up to anything.

Finally, we all know I don't engage in BS income claim marketing, but I increased revenue by at least 20% once I started selling strategy. It was a turning point for me revenue-wise.

I can't guarantee the same will happen for you, but the reality is that people will pay more for strategy than execution.

If you're not sure about selling strategy, here's three patterns you should watch for in your business.

Pattern #1: You Give Away the Strategy to Impress and Attract Clients

I fell into this first pattern during my early years as a freelancer. I wanted to prove to my potential clients that I was smart and knew what I was doing. I found myself overperforming in consulting calls trying to impress them with ideas of how we could work together. A big problem for me was that I'd get super excited as I chatted with a potential client and then get carried away with sharing the strategy I saw for them.

I will never be someone to squash your enthusiasm, but any strategy talk should be saved for when they're paying you. This is hard-won wisdom, and I can't tell you how many times I served up strategy on a consult call or in a proposal, and then the client had everything they needed to execute it in-house.

Pattern #2: You Don't Notice that You Aren't Charging for Strategy

This next one I see a lot with my clients when I first work with them as they overlook the value of strategy to their clients. They simply do the strategy work, buried within more tactical work.

The client doesn't necessarily know you're doing strategy work as they're not paying for it, and you're relegated to the role of "implementer."

I remember one client I had back when I wasn't focused on leading with strategy, and that relationship was so frustrating to me because they kept hiring other people for strategy. I felt overlooked and unappreciated as I watched them spend thousands of dollars on strategy work that I could have and should have been doing. Not to mention, I spent much time being paid way less than they were to fix their crappy work.

Pattern #3: You're Working with Clients Who Don't Value Strategy

You've probably had this happen to you. You're telling a prospective or current client they need strategy and they tell you that they don't need it. Or they're "good" and have it covered.

This would happen to me periodically when I was doing copywriting work, as people would want me to write web copy without a strategy. Before I made it a required part of my copywriting process, I would do it for them, as it's impossible to write copy without a content strategy for the website.

I was doing hours of essentially free strategy work as they didn't value strategy and wouldn't pay for it. It would be easy for me to blame clients for this, but I didn't educate them that a content strategy is essential to writing website copy.

When you have a strategy offering for clients, you're able to break these patterns. You're selling to the type of client who values strategy, pays for it, and ultimately sees you as being a strategic partner rather than just a tactical implementer in their business.

That's the power of selling strategy. It shifts how you show up in your business, how you deliver your services, and how your clients see you.

This sounds good, but now you're probably thinking: *how do I do this?* That's precisely why I created Sell the Strategy®, as you need a framework to help you implement this in your business.

WHAT IS SELL THE STRATEGY®?

Put simply, Sell the Strategy® is a proven method to help you put strategy *first* in your offers. To help you get paid for your experience and strategic thinking so you can reach your goals.

Sell the Strategy® is more than you having a signature service or method. It's about getting to the heart of what your client needs and is really willing to pay for.

Too many times, signature services (and how they're taught) package up a bunch of crap or are too focused on the service provider's needs. Or let's be real, it's a big old cash grab with an overpriced offer that no one really needs.

Sell the Strategy® is client-centric and is really about finding the sweet spot between what strategy you can bring, and what your clients really and truly need.

You may do this in some way right now, or not at all. Sell the Strategy® focuses on the strategy being the core of your offering, not execution. Even if you do tactical work, it positions those services in a way that's higher value, not just transactional task completion.

When creating a specific product around the strategy work you're already doing, the process I have built revolves around these five elements or steps: product, position, price, promotion, and prepare. (You may remember some of these from Chapter 9 - but here they're specific to Sell the Strategy®)

Product: What is Your Strategy Offer?

The first step to figure out is your product. What are you going to do for your strategy offering? Hint: this is probably something you're already doing, it just needs to be packaged and sold more specifically as being strategy-focused.

Your strategy offer needs to be carefully designed to fill a real need in the market and fit into your overall offer suite. This is something you likely already do, but it's hidden away or not recognized for the value it brings.

This combines your skills, talents, processes, and target market into a clear strategy package with transparent processes.

The product development process requires market research and validation, followed by outlining the product and nailing down your signature process.

Position: Why Will People Buy From You?

The strategy product you create above is only one part of this. You need to be able to explain it too and have a unique value proposition. The reason your strategy offers a unique value proposition is so people know why it's different, why they need it, and why they should choose you.

Without this, you'll struggle to sell your offer, as people need to see the problem you solve and the results you can deliver.

Price: How Much Will You Charge?

People pay for strategy, so you need to charge accordingly. You need to price your strategy offer in a way that articulates the value of what you're delivering. Pricing your strategy offer should consider your target client and industry, current market position, and more.

Also, your strategy offer should be priced intentionally based on how you want to show up in the market and how it fits with your other services.

Your price needs to reflect that this is transformational, not transactional work. (More on pricing coming up in the next chapter.)

Promotion: How Will People Learn About It?

Next, you need a way to promote your strategy offering. Without promotion, it's going to languish on your website. Often, you'll need to build thought leadership around your Sell the Strategy® offer so that people really and truly get it.

That promotion part is like how I'm sharing the Sell the Strategy® Method now so that people start to see how this could help their business.

Having a strategic offer is one thing, but you need to be able to sell it. You need a promotional plan to keep it top of mind, so people know about it and want to work with you. Establishing your expertise around the offer and educating people about the problem you solve is key.

Prepare: The Nuts and Bolts of Delivery

The final step in the process is ensuring you have all your processes around your strategy offer in order. This includes everything from your intake form, to your client pre-work, to the templates you use to deliver the final product to clients, to your proposal descriptions, and more.

The client experience around your strategy offer is essential as you're commanding prices that require an elevated, professional delivery.

WILL SELLING STRATEGY WORK FOR ME?

You're probably starting to think of the possibilities for what you could do by putting strategy first. Or how you can do a better job of positioning the strategic work you already do.

And now you're thinking, but will this work for me?

The answer is, most likely, yes. I've worked with coaches, creatives, and consultants using the Sell the Strategy® approach for over five years. As service providers, we *all* do strategy work whether we sell it or not.

I've personally used this very effectively with corporate clients and small businesses, both B2B and in the online business market. I've sold many different strategic offers to clients and there are countless ways to package it up, including audits, playbooks, strategic plans, intensives, and much, much more.

The possibilities are nearly endless, and the real key to selling the strategy is understanding what your clients value along with the strategic thinking they need to be successful.

Challenges With Selling Strategy

Perhaps you've already been selling strategy, or maybe you're not even sure where to start. Let's look at some of the challenges that can occur for solo business owners.

Scenario #1: You're Not Selling Strategy, But You're Ready To

Maybe you know you're ready to sell strategy. I've sold you on its value, but you're unsure where to start.

Step one for any strategy offer is looking at where the strategy may be hiding in your current services. When I work with my clients on this, we're always looking for something they're already doing that can be packaged up as a strategy offer.

Sometimes it's something they do all the time that's not seen as strategy. Other times, it's something they do in their processes that clients don't know about but which is incredibly valuable.

My top recommendation is that you don't try to rush this. You can't force this into existence, so if it's not immediately obvious, give it some time to percolate.

Trust me when I say this. At some point, that strategy package is going to be right there in front of you. You may be tempted to decide it's way too simple, but the most impactful strategy offer *is* going to be simple.

It's hard to sell anything complicated. You want your offer to be something people learn about and think, *"It's me! I have that problem. Sign me up."*

Notice I mentioned the problem? You need to be solving a real problem that your target client has. It may not be something they're lying in bed thinking about, but they need to have a real need, or you're going to struggle to sell to them.

As part of nailing down a strategy offer, you need to look at your potential clients, the current market, your competition, and more. Using myself as an example, I did a lot of research for Sell the Strategy® to ensure it was something that was actually needed and that solved a tangible set of problems. (Yes, I know it's meta that my strategy offer is to help people create their strategy offers.)

Once you have the product nailed down, you'll want to focus on the positioning. Don't skip this step. You need to be able to identify where you fit in the market and why you're different, or you're going to find yourself struggling with your promotion.

Speaking of promotion, don't fall into the trap of magical thinking: that if you create it, they will come. As I've shared multiple times, promotion is as critical as how you package and position the offer. If you don't have the right promotional plan, or the willingness to actually get it out there, your strategy package will languish on your website.

Finally, consider your pricing. It's okay to start with an intro price and raise it over time as you refine your strategy offer.

Scenario #2. The Strategy Package Isn't Selling

If you've never sold your package, get curious about why that may be. Something I often see in the market is products that are created based on what the business owner wants, not what the market wants.

The best strategy offer is in the sweet spot between your skills and experience, and the problems your potential clients have. If you find you have to do an extraordinary amount of education about the existence of the problem, consider how you're positioning the offer or if you need to simplify it. Look at each product element and its positioning to consider what could be refined.

Also, if you get good feedback on the offer but there's a pricing objection, you may need to adjust your pricing to put it within reach of your target market.

Finally, consider your promotion. Strategy is not a quick fix. The promotion you need to educate people about the offer and how you can help takes time. If you're likely to get frustrated and quit after sharing it three times, you need to get a promotion plan in place.

Scenario #3. You're Not Selling Enough Strategy

Maybe you've sold some strategy packages and you've truly validated that people want this offer, but you want to sell *more* of them.

First, I want you to consider if you're being realistic. If you're selling eight strategy packages a year right now, and it's your highest-priced offer, it can be tempting to do the math and be like, *"Great, I just need to sell two per month or 24 per year."*

Can you really deliver that many packages? Start with nailing down a realistic plan for how many strategy packages you can handle per month or year.

Next, you need to define a realistic bump in what "more strategy packages" means based on your current marketing and promotion.

You may need to step up your promotional plan for your strategy and add something new, as your current audience may already be fatigued with the offer.

The lack of a solid promotional plan for your strategy offer is usually a big reason why you're not selling it. You need eyeballs from new potential clients, and that may require you to do more or different types of marketing activities.

This is an excellent example of promotional activity. Since launching Sell the Strategy® as an intensive, I've had a plan in place to periodically focus on promotion for it. During those periods, I talk about it on my podcast, in my emails, and on Instagram.

I don't just expect people to know it exists. I talk about it in promotional sprints at different times during the year.

Shifting gears, you've worked with several clients on your strategy offer, so you have feedback and intelligence to help refine it. You know it works, but you have an opportunity to improve it.

Questions to consider in refining your strategy offer:

- Do I need to adjust or update elements of the offer?
- How can I better share the value?

- Is my positioning solid, or do I need to speak to the problem differently?
- Is my price point right? Does it need to increase or be reconsidered?
- Am I getting the right clients in the door with this offer?

Carefully assessing your strategy offer, and making updates as you learn more about your clients and your process, is critical. This feedback cycle enables you to improve upon what you're doing.

DON'T SLEEP ON SELLING STRATEGY

Remember Emily Gertenbach, the SEO strategist and content writer we met in Chapter 3? When we were working together in 2023, she was offering strategy services, but hadn't really productized it as a strategy offer. In our sessions, we devised the Stress-Free SEO Strategy for her business, which enabled her to not only position herself as a consultant, but price and promote the service in a way that was incredibly enticing to her potential clients.

In the first six months of 2024, Emily had booked eight of these strategy clients, which helped reinforce her expert positioning in the market while boosting her revenue.

This is a great example of why you shouldn't sleep on selling strategy. It offers a proven and systematic approach to breaking your income ceiling, and being seen as the expert you truly are.

CHAPTER 12

WHy Not an Agency?

Author's Note: If you've never been interested in growing an agency, you may want to skip ahead to Chapter 13. You can always come back to it, if and when you feel any sort of pull towards the agency business model.

You may be wondering why I'm evangelizing about staying solo, when I actually run a content marketing agency called Scoop Studios.

The answer is very simple. Too many solo business owners become accidental agency owners as they feel like there's no other option for them to continue growing. *Staying Solo*® offers multiple proven strategies and tactics for business owners to build a business with a solid foundation — without feeling like they have no other choice than to build an agency.

Starting and growing an agency is hard. It's much harder than anyone ever realizes. It's far more complex than just hiring some people and watching the cash roll in.

I've spent my entire career working either as an agency employee, freelancer, or agency owner, which gives me a depth of experience I simply don't see amid these big, bold, brash promises about what an agency can do for you. Even though I had years of experience working in and with agencies, I didn't even know what I was in for.

That's why I want you to know that you don't have to start an agency. You can use everything discussed in the prior chapters to grow in a simple and sustainable way.

Building an agency should be a strategic choice, not something you choose to do lightly.

WHAT TO CONSIDER: SOLO OR AGENCY

First, let's start with my definitions so we're all on the same page. While it's not uncommon for solo business owners to grow into agency owners, there's a marked difference in how business is done and delivered on an ongoing basis.

If you look at the key areas of your business, each one is quite different.

Marketing and Sales

Many solo business owners run very successful businesses with minimal marketing as they have limited capacity. To build an agency, you need to be able to bring in more clients and manage more complex projects to cover your team and infrastructure costs, and turn a profit.

With that in mind, many agency owners don't consider that the marketing needs to evolve and may require more thought leadership or proactive marketing. One of the biggest mistakes I made as an agency owner in the early days was thinking that my lead sources as a solopreneur would be sufficient to fill my pipeline when I shifted to the agency model.

Going from a team of one to an agency with four full-time employees was a wake-up call regarding the lead gen and marketing level needed.

None of that is to say you can't have a thriving agency, but there's a distinct uplevel that eventually has to happen with marketing when growing an agency.

Along with the marketing comes the potential for more sales activity, which can be time-consuming.

Many of the most successful agency owners I know actually love the marketing and sales part of the role, which is ideal as they can focus on that while their team does the client work on a day-to-day basis.

The final thing I want to touch on related to sales is that your pricing needs to be higher with an agency than when you're a solopreneur. If you're in an industry where you constantly find yourself at the high end of the market, you may need to look for new ways to serve clients who will pay the price you need to charge to cover the hard costs of agency operations.

Client Service and Deliverables

For many solo business owners, one of the appeals of moving to the agency model is that they won't have to handle all the client service and deliverables. While I get this, I want to be clear that having a team doesn't mean you don't do client work anymore. You might just do less of it over time, and you have the support of your team in getting things out the door.

Over the past seven years, I've done less and less client work, but make no mistake, I still do client work most weeks. I'm involved with our clients and deliverables. Getting to this point has been a process as the team has changed over time.

I'll talk more about the leadership and team aspects of running an agency in a moment, but I don't want anyone jumping into this business model thinking they won't be doing any client work and will be sitting on the beach three months from now.

Ultimately, your name is on the door, and your company's reputation is at stake, so you have a vested interest in ensuring clients are happy and that your team is delivering as expected.

There's also the shift from "me" to "we," which requires getting your clients on board with other team members. While this is doable, it can be tricky as you need your client to trust your team like they trust you. In doing that, there's absolutely a cost involved, as you need to lay the groundwork for everyone and support it with clear agency standards.

For clients who are used to working exclusively with you, this can be a painful (and annoying) process as you wean them off depending only on you, especially as they're likely paying more now that you have a team.

A final cost related to clients that can be surprising is how client expectations can rise with the agency model. As a solo business owner, your clients likely perceive you differently than they will when you have an agency. This makes managing client expectations and demands critical as you grow. Otherwise, you'll fall into a pattern of overservicing them to keep them happy.

In all honesty, if you're someone who currently struggles with keeping clients happy, client expectations, and boundaries, moving to a team-based model won't fix it. That's the kind of thing that should be handled before you start bringing other people into the mix, or you have the potential to set yourself up for chaos.

Leadership

The conversation about building an agency frequently skips over the leadership part of the equation. It's all about the benefits, but it fails to address that you need to be ready to lead when you have an agency, whether you have a team of three or 30.

Leadership skills can be learned and developed of course, but staying solo may be your best choice if this is less appealing.

For me, leadership was something I resisted after leading a team when I worked in an agency. With a small child and a new business as a freelancer, there was zero appeal in having a team. I didn't want to have to spend my time on feedback, coaching, and more. I only decided to move towards having an agency once my kid was 11 years old and I had been running my business for 10 years.

Part of this comes down to how you want to spend your time. One option may be more appealing than the other for you right now. An agency is a viable choice if you want to focus on leadership and business development. Conversely, that may differ from how you want to spend your time.

Remember, saying yes to one option doesn't mean it's a no to the other forever.

THE PERSONAL COST OF AGENCY OWNERSHIP

Do you remember how it felt when you started your business?

You were probably excited but also had a neverending to-do list and were working a lot. Creating an agency doesn't require you to start from square one, but you'll have a new set of demands on your time and energy.

Any new phase of your business will require an upfront invest-ment of your time. I encourage you to consider if this is the right move for you in this season and how moving to an agency model has the potential to impact your personal life.

Any shift to an agency will require you to develop new skills, and have the energetic and emotional capacity to do so. Just like dealing with clients in those early days of your business, the interpersonal aspects of building your agency's team can be equally challenging.

Please keep in mind that there are many positives to working as part of a team, and it can be incredibly rewarding. Fostering people's professional growth, including their skills and confidence, has been one of my biggest career highlights.

On the flip side, there's the potential for immense stress related to being responsible for other people's livelihoods and managing the financial risks of your agency. While you have a team around you, shouldering these burdens can be isolating, so it's critical that you have ongoing support.

Jules Taggart intentionally built her marketing agency Wayward Kind, but in 2022 opted to pivot back to being a solo business owner: "There were a lot of things during COVID that fueled growth. I looked around and took a breath and asked myself if this is what I wanted to do for the rest of my life. It wasn't doing great things for my mental health."

BENEFITS: STAYING SOLO® VS AGENCY BUSINESS MODEL

No matter which business model you choose, you don't have to stop being a service provider and instead start running courses and programs. Despite what celebrity entrepreneurs say, countless people like the service business model, and it offers a viable and proven path.

Here are the key benefits of each approach.

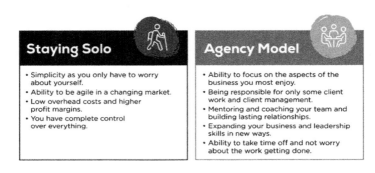

Staying Solo	Agency Model
• Simplicity as you only have to worry about yourself. • Ability to be agile in a changing market. • Low overhead costs and higher profit margins. • You have complete control over everything.	• Ability to focus on the aspects of the business you most enjoy. • Being responsible for only some client work and client management. • Mentoring and coaching your team and building lasting relationships. • Expanding your business and leadership skills in new ways. • Ability to take time off and not worry about the work getting done.

MICRO AGENCIES: A SUSTAINABLE OPTION

At some point, an agency may well be the natural and most strategic next step for you. However, this doesn't mean you have to go from being solo to having a team of 15 and building something big.

Micro agencies offer a unique opportunity for service businesses to grow in a way that blends the best parts of an agency and a lifestyle business.

A micro agency is a service business operating as an agency with a small team of employees and/or contractors. Typically "micro" refers to less than 10 employees.

The SoDA & Productive: The Global Agency Landscape 2022 report, which surveyed leaders in agencies of all sizes from around the globe, gives some insight into how well agencies are performing.

Of particular note is the fact that this data is from what I consider micro agencies, with 31% having less than $1 million USD in revenue and 36% falling between $1 and $5 million per year. The report shared that in 2021, 44% of agencies reported revenue growth of 25% or more, and 51% shared that it was a banner year for their firm.

In the report's key findings, they discuss how agencies adapted quickly to the new realities of work, which isn't surprising when you consider that over 50% of the agencies who participated are micro agencies.

From my point of view, micro agencies have the best of both worlds. There's a proven business model, but we can evolve quickly in response to market conditions, as well as changing client needs.

INTENTIONAL GROWTH OF A MICRO AGENCY

Every business owner knows that growth is never linear. Sometimes, it's so far from a straight line that you wonder if you're doing something wrong.

Starting and growing a micro agency is one of the most rewarding and challenging things I've ever done. If you're an agency owner, you know exactly what I'm talking about. And if you're newer on your agency path, you're about to discover what I'm talking about!

When you start an agency, you typically have a handful of clients and a vision for how you no longer want to be a team of one. As you grow your agency, you will likely find that reality differs from your initial vision.

The shift from being a solo business owner to building a micro agency isn't always a clear and intentional choice. Sometimes, it's even accidental; we hire a contractor or two, then suddenly we're not a one-person show anymore and slowly become an agency.

This is often where a lot of strife occurs, as in this scenario, we may need a clearer idea of our goals, profit margins, and how we will grow.

If this sounds like you, please keep in mind this isn't "bad" per se, but rather it may be the root of some of the challenges you face as you grow.

On the flip side, even if you have a perfect five-year plan for your agency, things shift and change over time.

This is why every agency owner must continuously focus on defining growth goals. As I've said, that may sound obvious, but the truth is even with a micro agency, the goals may vary wildly based on the owner's vision and objectives.

In some cases, it may be to have a limited client roster and to cap growth at a specific level; in others, it may be continuing to grow year-over-year.

No matter how you may approach it, you need to have a plan for a sustainable path to growth.

Here are a few questions to explore related to your growth goals for a potential micro agency:

- How big do I want my team to be? My client roster?
- How much time do I want to invest in the agency and its growth?
- What revenue level feels sustainable and profitable?
- What do I want the agency to look like three to five years from now?

Don't overthink your answers. My goal here is to get you thinking about the micro agency model in a way where it's not just about growth for the sake of growth, but rather building something that works for you and your life.

TOUGH TRUTHS ABOUT MICRO AGENCY GROWTH

Earlier in this book, I discussed revenue break points where businesses struggle to grow at specific points due to the skills and resources needed.

I want to explore that a bit more, as it helps frame up what it's like to grow a micro agency and what may be needed for you to execute your goals. I don't think we talk about this part enough, so we end up thinking that our growth should be linear.

I found it frustrating when growth wasn't happening in a straight line in my agency. Once I realized that the time and money required to add on more clients (and revenue) had a lag effect, I was much more confident in my ability to grow and sustain my business over time.

I want to avoid being prescriptive here, as experiences will vary wildly. It would be easy for me to say, "With an agency with $250k in annual revenue, you'll need a full-time employee and likely have less than ten clients."

The key is to watch for where things are stuck. No matter what you do, your revenue starts to plateau when you're unable to take on more clients due to a lack of resources, or needing to uplevel systems and processes within the agency.

This isn't necessarily a *bad* thing. It's important information to help you guide what's next and decide if you will continue to grow, and if so, how fast.

When evaluating this, you need to decide if you're willing, and frankly able, to make the investments required and take the potential hit to your profit margin. Also, you need to ensure that you're not "investing" when you don't have a clear and proven way to get the clients you need to expand your revenue.

Consider these questions when you're deciding on your next move:

- What's needed to facilitate further growth?
- Do you have the time, capacity, and money to make that investment?
- What's the current state of your client roster? Do you have more clients currently than you can handle? Do you have a proven, consistent way of acquiring new leads?
- What happens if you don't grow anymore? What happens if you do?
- What's your number one reason for wanting to grow to the next stage?
- What will you gain professionally and personally? What will you sacrifice?

This may seem like a lot to process, but part of a sustainable business is ensuring you carefully assess when and how to grow — and when to stay where you are.

MICRO AGENCY PITFALLS TO WATCH FOR

A common thread with my clients and community is that they strive to run an ethical, profitable, sustainable business. The micro agency owners I work with are no exception, as they're committed to doing what's right for their clients and teams.

That can lead to challenges you may not expect, so let's talk about possible pitfalls if you pursue micro agency ownership.

Not Compromising Quality

When you're a solo business owner, you have a firm handle on all your client deliverables, but that changes when you have a team. It can be demanding as you have a more extensive client roster and team to ensure that everything meets your stringent quality standards.

This is not to say that you need to ensure perfection, but a major mistake I've seen too many times to count is that the bigger an agency grows, the more quality slips. That's not to say it's a given, but growing too quickly can compromise quality.

Overextending Your Finances

Growth can quickly impact your cash flow, and expanding can strain your finances. The key is taking calculated risks and not engaging in magical thinking where you overextend your finances in pursuit of growth.

The definition of "overextended" differs for each of us, but I encourage you to make these decisions methodically. Not every problem can be solved by throwing money at it, mainly when there's reliance on outside factors, such as signing new clients that aren't even in the pipeline yet.

Expecting Too Much From Your Team

When growing your agency, you need to be conscious of the needs and limitations of your team. No matter how amazing they may be, you have to remember they'll never be as invested in growth as you're going to be. That may sound harsh, but we simply can't expect them to be ready or willing to do the same things we would.

Growth plans need to be managed so that it's not just about what you want but what's best for the team. Your team's well-being is essential to ongoing success and shouldn't be sacrificed due to a personal need to expand relentlessly.

Sticking to Your Values

So many of us start businesses because we want to do things differently and are deeply committed to our values. That said, the pursuit of growth, even in a micro agency, can put our values to the test.

Challenges will arise from potential clients we're unsure about, approaches to our work that we're not aligned with, and much more. As always, I'm not going to tell you what to do, but I will say I've never regretted making decisions that result in less revenue or slower growth when I know those decisions are aligned.

Sometimes, you'll need to make choices at the expense of your bottom line. You can make this easier by developing a documented set of values and principles that guide your business decisions. This acts as a north star in challenging situations and ensures you make the right choice.

IS AN AGENCY A CHOICE YOU SHOULD CONSIDER?

There are many compelling reasons to start an agency, but remember, my goal is to ensure that anyone who goes down this path is making an informed decision.

When I asked Tressa Beheim, who owns an operations services agency, about the pros and cons of running an agency from her perspective, here's what she shared:

"A big plus of the agency model is the level of support we can provide to clients. I'm able to focus on strategy and consulting, which is my strength, and not get caught up in execution. Plus, I'm able to travel and take time off without worrying like I did as a solo business owner.

I've definitely learned that growing an agency is a long-term project as everything takes way longer than you think, even if you're delegating it. As a leader, you need to be prepared for the operating costs of an agency. Despite what people say about hiring, it's going to cost way more than you probably think.

If you hate marketing and business development, you may find running an agency challenging as it's an ongoing priority because you have a team to pay. You'll always be balancing that with client service."

My experience has been similar to Tressa since I started my agency in 2016. It's a big reason that over time I've chosen to streamline my team and services.

If you're a solo business owner who's intrigued by the agency business model as a possibility for your business, I encourage you to check out my podcast *Confessions of a Micro Agency Owner* where we talk about all of this. You can find it on Apple Podcasts, Spotify, or wherever you get your podcasts.

Chapter 13

The Business of Boundaries

What I've shared with you so far in this book is designed to provide you with a realistic path to simplicity and sustainability as a solo service business owner. But there's one final element that's essential for anyone working with clients.

Boundaries.

Boundaries will make or break your ability to build a simple and sustainable business using the strategies outlined above. From draining your time and energy to wreaking havoc on your mental health and bottom line, poor boundaries can turn your business into a nightmare.

While it's easy to complain about clients, we've got a critical role to play. Setting boundaries is not just about reacting when someone's already trampled all over them; it's about laying out the rules of engagement from day one and making sure everyone's on the same page.

Having boundaries is essential as a service business owner. And not just with nightmare clients from the fiery pits of hell (you know the ones that make you question your choice to run a business in the first place), but with all of our clients.

WHAT ARE BOUNDARIES WITH CLIENTS?

One of my biggest pet peeves is when people use boundaries as a way to avoid actually serving their clients. That's not what boundaries are at all, despite what that celebrity entrepreneur may pretend.

So, what are boundaries? Boundaries with clients are the limits and guidelines that you, as a service provider, use to establish a professional relationship with them. The goal of these boundaries is to ensure a respectful relationship that works for everyone.

Your boundaries should help you balance serving client needs with protecting your well-being, schedule, and business interests.

Your client boundaries may include communication, time commitments, scope of work, deadlines, pricing, payments, and even professional conduct. Clearly defining expectations of how you work together creates healthy working relationships with your clients.

When you have weak, unclear, or non-existent boundaries, multiple aspects of your business may be impacted. Bad boundaries with your clients always come at a cost.

COMMON EXAMPLES OF BAD CLIENT BOUNDARIES

If you've ever struggled with bad client boundaries, I want you to know it's completely normal.

Service business owners may struggle with boundaries at different stages of their business, or even on an ongoing basis. Even as a very experienced service provider, on occasion I find myself needing a refresher.

Your boundaries are a constant work in progress, so here are a few areas you may need to strengthen them.

Availability

How available are you to your clients? You need to have set hours of work and not fall into the trap of being constantly or even inappropriately available.

Yes, that means not tapping out that reply email while at your kid's soccer game on a Sunday morning. If you say you'll reply to a client email within 48 hours during the working week, then replying on your day off is training your clients to think you're available all the time.

Personal Space Invasion

Do you allow your clients to intrude on your personal time? Call or message you outside of your work hours? Ask for you to work on the weekend or even on your vacation?

Scope Creep/Overservicing

It's really easy to fall into the trap of overservicing your clients or not sticking to the scope of work. There's a difference between the occasional exception and constantly providing work for free.

Underpricing

Pricing your services too low on a consistent basis is a boundary issue. Whatever the reason you undercharge, you need to be aware of how this impacts you over time. You don't owe anyone a "deal" and it's okay to get a no from a potential client.

Communication

Your clients should be aware of how to best communicate with you, provide feedback, and so forth. This is actually of benefit to them, as if they're DMing you on Instagram, WhatsApping you on the weekend, and using other methods to try to get hold of you, something might get missed.

As a service provider you want to be proactive with communicating timelines and progress.

Overpromising

Do you fall into the trap of agreeing to unrealistic deadlines? Or saying yes to things you don't have any business doing? Before you make any promise to deliver something, you need to consider how it will impact you.

Difficulty Saying No

People pleasers unite! If you can't say no to work from clients, or requests, or anything else, you need to learn how.

Failing to Enforce Boundaries

Once you set boundaries, you need to stick to them. From payments to late fees, to deadlines, to communication channels, you need to take your own medicine.

Accepting Disrespectful Behaviour

Tolerating disrespectful or abusive behaviour from clients instead of establishing boundaries for professional conduct.

Building a service business that actually serves you, and is sustainable, relies on you having these client boundaries handled.

THE REAL COST OF POOR CLIENT BOUNDARIES

When you think about your client boundaries, it's easy to fall into the trap of going along to get along. There are so many times we decide that it's easier to just accept how things are with our clients versus taking proactive steps to change it.

I'm far from perfect in my client relationships. While I generally don't have a problem with boundaries, sometimes I decide I don't have the time, energy, or emotional capacity to deal with resetting boundaries with a client. But then I realize that if I don't handle it, it's going to cost me.

When you think about the cost of "bad" boundaries, you may struggle to pin down exactly what they are as so many times they're intangible. It's hard to put a number on how you're feeling when a client asks for one more thing, or you don't like a client's tone.

Yet, there are some boundaries where it's easier to understand the consequences, especially the ones related to your time and money.

Underpricing

For example, when we underprice our services, or do work for free, we're devaluing our precious time. Typically we don't set out to do these things, but charging too little, or allowing too many extras to sneak into a project, accumulates over time.

Maybe you have a long-term client whose retainer is priced at your rate from three years ago. Every week, every month, that cost adds up and it's impacting your revenue. You could be working with another client that has a clearer scope of work at a higher rate.

Scope Creep

Scope creep is a tangible (and very common) cost of weak client boundaries. If you're constantly overservicing your clients, they're eating away at time you could be using for other client projects, while degrading your hourly rate or overall revenue.

Honestly, scope creep is one of the trickiest boundaries as you may barely notice it. I recommend a time-tracking exercise if you're not sure where your time is going and suspect you may have scope creep going on.

If you're constantly over budget with your clients and not charging them for those services, it's costing you. This is a persistent problem for many service business owners, but it's one you absolutely want to get a handle on.

Payment Policies

You should have a non-negotiable boundary around your payments from clients as this can too easily lead to cash flow problems. Having clear payment policies that you establish from day one with clients is essential. Your contracts should include contingencies for late payments, withholding deliverables, or stopping work, as you don't want to find yourself in a situation where a client defaults on paying you for work performed.

Infringing on Personal Time

This cost is self-explanatory, and even if you don't mind, it costs you. Work interjects into your non-work time, and that takes up valuable real estate in your head. Also, this can lead to you feeling resentful of, or frustrated or disrespected by, your clients, which impacts your working relationship.

If this is an issue for you, consider communicating your availability, office hours, and standard response times. Then, don't breach your own boundaries; if you want clients to stick to them, you need to do the same.

Deadlines and Timelines

Every service business owner knows that failing to manage deadlines and timelines with clients can come with a hefty price tag. Your boundaries around deadlines and timelines impact your productivity and profitability.

If you have a client who constantly misses deadlines to provide you with input on a project but then wants you to turn around work quickly, that has a material impact on your schedule. And it has the potential to cost you time that you could be spending working on other projects.

Your clients judge you on your ability to deliver on time, so constantly managing expectations on deadlines or timelines ensures things go smoothly.

Keep in mind that it's entirely reasonable for you to set out boundaries around any changes to the timeline as part of your contracts. This may be charging fees for project delays or rebooking fees to help ensure you're not held hostage by a client's choice to stretch things out.

Communication

Finally, communication serves as a crucial boundary tied to time management. It's all about setting up clear guidelines regarding the how, when, and why you connect with clients.

If you're a designer and you communicate with clients via your project management system, you need to ensure they stick to that plan. You don't want them emailing you and DM-ing you on Instagram. Fragmented communications suck up energy and time as you try to corral everything.

One communications boundary I've had to put in place in my agency is how we receive feedback on our work. We ask that clients provide feedback via comments and/or tracked edits in Google Docs, instead of asking for a phone call to review live.

These types of boundaries ultimately prevent you from constant interruptions and time wasters throughout your day.

THE HIDDEN COSTS OF BROKEN BOUNDARIES

Time- and money-related costs of bad boundaries are the easiest to quantify, but what about the less tangible ones?

Yes, I'm talking about personal costs like emotional exhaustion, drained energy, and even impact on your self-esteem. Or the resentment that builds when you're working on a client's "emergency" request when you were supposed to be spending time with friends or family.

Honestly, many times you may not even realize the toll the lack of boundaries are taking on you over time.

When you think about your capacity, you likely immediately think about your available time to do client work, but not your energetic, emotional, and sensory capacity. Perhaps you have a client who's always crossing your boundaries, and it's fine until one day it's finally not and you're ready to fire them as a client.

If you find yourself constantly feeling resentful, frustrated, irritated, stressed, or anxious due to your client work, that may be a sign that you need to adjust or enforce your boundaries. Being complacent or avoidant will only allow these feelings to accumulate over time.

No matter how you may be feeling, there's always an opportunity to set or reset boundaries with your clients. The last thing you want is for this to worsen over time so it's bleeding over into how you feel about yourself, or placing a strain on your interpersonal relationships.

That's where you really start to see the cost of not setting boundaries with clients. You may experience a loss of motivation, resentment of your work or clients, and feel like you're compromising your values, ethics, or professional integrity.

No client is ever going to be worth it. While you need to make a living, there will always be another way to generate revenue that doesn't come with such steep costs.

From my point of view, one of the biggest reasons service business owners end up burnt out can be chalked up to not having strong enough boundaries.

Constantly overextending yourself and letting people violate your boundaries (or simply not having any boundaries at all) is a recipe for burnout. And I don't mean burnout in the way that people talk about online where they need a day off, but true, persistent burnout.

Burnout is a state of emotional, mental, and physical exhaustion that can't be fixed with a few days off.

If you're feeling cynical, perpetually exhausted, and like doing your work is a struggle, you may be experiencing burnout. I'm by no means an expert on this topic, but this is a true cost of bad boundaries with clients.

Signs you may be experiencing burnout include feeling:

- Depleted despite adequate rest and sleep.
- Detached or disconnected from your work.
- Like your performance is declining and you can't meet commitments.

Boundaries aren't the only way to address burnout, but they're a critical component of being able to ensure that you don't find yourself in a constant cycle of recovery and burnout.

Even if you're not feeling burnt out, your boundaries with clients are critical to the sustainability of your service business.

HOW TO SET BOUNDARIES WITH CLIENTS

Setting boundaries with your clients isn't just about putting up barriers; it's about keeping your well-being intact while making sure your bank account doesn't take a hit.

It's an essential skill, and no matter where you may be right now with boundaries, you can always set new ones, revamp existing ones, or find new ways to uphold them. A professional setting functions better with clear boundaries, and you can be of service to your clients *and* have rock solid boundaries.

The ideal situation is that you set boundaries with your clients from day one in your proposals, contracts, and onboarding, and then stick to them throughout your working relationship. When you breach your boundaries, you signal to your clients that it's okay for them to do the same.

What if you're already working with clients and you've not done a great job of setting boundaries so far?

You can set new boundaries at any point in the relationship, as you might often feel frustrated with clients when you don't take the time to lay out the rules of engagement from the start. When setting a new boundary, you need to communicate it clearly, and you can do it in a kind, factual manner.

On the flip side, what about when your clients are aware of a boundary, but they're not sticking to it? Start by assessing if this is a one-time thing, or if they have a pattern of just doing whatever they want.

In the event of a pattern of breached boundaries, there are three ways to handle it depending on the situation. You can remind them of the boundary, or take the time to restate it so there's no confusion. Many times that will be enough to get things back on track.

The other option is redirecting your client so they're no longer engaging in that action. For example, if you have a client that constantly emails you instead of communicating with you in your project management system, you can remind them and then consistently only communicate with them via the proper channels.

Finally, there will be instances with clients where you've done everything possible to get them to respect your boundaries, and they don't care. They just keep doing whatever they want.

The question you need to consider is how much the breached boundary costs you. Is it sucking up time, wasting money, stressing you out, or draining your energy. Is that worth it?

If the answer is yes, you'll need to take more concrete action to reset expectations with your client. This may require you to modify how you manage them on a day-to-day basis. If the answer is that it's not worth it, I want to remind you that there are no bonus points for continuing to work with a client that's costing you in any way.

BE BRAVE WITH YOUR BOUNDARIES

Remember, your boundaries will always be a work in progress as long as you work with clients. Humans working with other humans will always have their challenges.

I've been working in client services my entire career, and I *still* have moments where my boundaries aren't as solid as I'd like them to be. The key is recognizing when you're wavering and getting back on track quickly.

To get extra support in building and holding your boundaries, there's a boundaries workshop and accompanying workbook included in the resources for this book. It's included in the Staying Solo Kit which you can sign up for at: www.stayingsolokit.com.

Chapter 14

Bigger Isn't Better

When you think about your business it's easy to fall into the trap of thinking that bigger automatically means better, especially when the prevailing message of entrepreneurship is that if you don't want to "scale" you're scared or playing small.

As humans, it's natural for us to compare ourselves to others as a way to figure out how we're doing, so when we only see examples of businesses that aren't like ours, we start to feel like we're "doing it wrong."

I want to remind you of the fact that the majority of businesses are solo, service-based businesses, so you're not an outlier.

You're the norm.

The status quo of entrepreneurship is overly focused on strategies and tactics that are both unrealistic and unsustainable for the majority of business owners, so it's time to throw away this rulebook and do things differently.

Remember why you started your business. It was probably to have more flexibility or be able to live your life in a certain way, so why the hell would you sacrifice that for a bullshit dream that's dictated to you by outside forces?

Screw that. You deserve a business and life that honors your values and well-being.

Throughout *Staying Solo*®, I've provided you with practical, proven ways to grow a business without having to grind yourself into the ground, so now it's time for you to go and put it into action.

You get to choose exactly how you do that, but treat this as a starting point to help you make it simpler, and much more sustainable.

MORE RESOURCES: The Staying Solo® Starter Kit

Throughout this book, I've shared resources to help you put this into action. I encourage you to sign up to get access to the Staying Solo® Starter Kit now.

In this free kit you'll get:

- Two pricing calculators
- Personal salary calculator
- Brave Boundaries workshop
- Purposeful Packages workshop
- Seasonal Planning workbook
- Exclusive podcast with stories of solo service business owners.
- Simple Lead Tracker

Sign up at: www.stayingsolokit.com.

Chapter 1:

Fuller, J., & Kerr, W. (2022, March 23). *The Great Resignation Didn't Start with the Pandemic.* Harvard Business Review. https://hbr. org/2022/03/the-great-resignation-didnt-start-with-the-pandemic

Penn, R., & Nezamis, E. (2022, June). Job openings and quits reach record highs in 2021, layoffs and discharges fall to record lows. *Monthly Labor Review.* U.S. Bureau of Labor Statistics. https://doi. org/10.21916/mlr.2022.17

Horsley, S. (2022, September 27). *Women are back in the workforce after leaving to caretake during the pandemic.* NPR. https://www.npr. org/2022/09/27/1125478595/women-are-back-in-the-workforce-after-leaving-to-caretake-during-the-pandemic

McKinsey & Company. (2021, March 8). *COVID-19's impact on women's employment.* https://www.mckinsey. com/featured-insights/diversity-and-inclusion/ seven-charts-that-show-covid-19s-impact-on-womens-employment

Masterson, V. (2022, July 20). *Here's what women's entrepreneurship looks like around the world.* The World Economic Forum. https://www. weforum.org/agenda/2022/07/women-entrepreneurs-gusto-gender/

Grossfeld, B. (2021, June 29). *Entrepreneurs Started Businesses in Record Numbers During the Pandemic.* The 360 Blog. https://www. salesforce.com/blog/small-business-pandemic-entrepreneurs/

O'Donnell, J., Newman, D., & Fikri, K. (2021, February 8). *The Startup Surge? Unpacking 2020 Trends in Business Formation.* Economic Innovation Group. https://eig.org/ the-startup-surge-business-formation-trends-in-2020/

U.S. Bureau of Labor Statistics. (2005, July 29). *The Economics Daily*. U.S. Department of Labour. https://www.bls.gov/opub/ted/2005/jul/wk4/art05.htm

Statista Research Department. (2024a, July 11). *Canada: number of self employed tax filers and dependents 2002-2022*. Statista. https://www.statista.com/statistics/484658/number-of-self-employed-taxfilers-and-dependents-in-canada/

Zhou, L. (2024, April 17). *How Many Americans Are Self-Employed? [2024 Data]*. Luisa Zhou. https://luisazhou.com/blog/how-many-americans-are-self-employed/

Main, K., & Bottorff, C. (2024, January 31). *Top Small Business Statistics of 2024*. Forbes Advisor. https://www.forbes.com/advisor/business/small-business-statistics/

GoDaddy Venture Forward & UCLA Anderson Forecast. (n.d.). *Microbusiness Activity Index*. Venture Forward. https://www.godaddy.com/ventureforward/explore-the-data/microbusiness-index/

Hartman, J., & Parilla, J. (2022, January 4). *Microbusinesses flourished during the pandemic. Now we must tap into their full potential*. The Brookings Institution. https://www.brookings.edu/articles/microbusinesses-flourished-during-the-pandemic-now-we-must-tap-into-their-full-potential/

Dunne, J. (2020, April 8). *"They should open it up": Why some small businesses have been shut out of COVID-19 emergency loan program*. CBC News. https://www.cbc.ca/news/business/small-business-loans-ceba-1.5526549

Parker, S. (2024, April 26). *Who Is the Richest Shark on 'Shark Tank'? A Look at the Cast's Net Worth.* TV Insider. https://www.tvinsider. com/gallery/richest-shark-on-shark-tank/#5

Pofeldt, E. (2019, July 29). *Million-Dollar, One-Person Business Revolution Accelerates.* Forbes. https://www.forbes.com/sites/ elainepofeldt/2019/06/27/million-dollar-one-person-business-revolution-accelerates/?sh=5486fade4526

Godlewski, N. (2023, January 23). *Small Business Revenue Statistics: Annual Sales and Earnings.* Fundera. https://www.fundera.com/ resources/small-business-revenue-statistics

Wood, M. (2020, November 11). *What Is the Average Small Business Owner Salary?* Fundera. https://www.fundera.com/blog/ study-finds-business-owners-earn-less

Hartmann, R. K., Spicer, A., & Krabbe, A. D. (2019, November 12). Towards an Untrepreneurial Economy? The Entrepreneurship Industry and the Rise of the Veblenian Entrepreneur. *Social Science Research Network.* https://dx.doi.org/10.2139/ssrn.3479042

Jones, C., & Spicer, A. (2009). *Unmasking the Entrepreneur.* Edward Elgar Publishing.

Bell, A., Chetty, R., Jaravel, X., Petkova, N., & Van Reenen, J. (2018, November 29). Who Becomes an Inventor in America? The Importance of Exposure to Innovation. *The Quarterly Journal of Economics, Volume 134*(Issue 2), 647-713. https://doi.org/10.1093/ qje/qjy028

Marinoni, A., & Voorheis, J. (2019). *Who Gains from Creative Destruction? Evidence from High-Quality Entrepreneurship in the United States.* IDEAS RePEc. https://ideas.repec.org/p/cen/wpaper/19-29.html

Hayward, M. L.A., Forster, W. R., Sarasvathy, S. D., & Fredrickson, B. L. (2010, November). Beyond hubris: How highly confident entrepreneurs rebound to venture again. *Journal of Business Venturing, Volume 25*(Issue 6), 569-578. https://doi.org/10.1016/j.jbusvent.2009.03.002

Pilat, D., & Krastev, S. (n.d.). *Why do we misjudge groups by only looking at specific group members?* The Decision Lab. https://thedecisionlab.com/biases/survivorship-bias

Hamilton, B. H. (2000, June). Does Entrepreneurship Pay? An Empirical Analysis of the Returns to Self-Employment. *Journal of Political Economy, Volume 108*(3), 604-631. https://doi.org/10.1086/262131

Delfino, D., & Shepard, D. (2024, April 8). *Percentage of Businesses That Fail — and How to Boost Chances of Success.* Lending Tree. https://www.lendingtree.com/business/small/failure-rate/

Carter, T., & Thomas, J. (2021, January 3). *The True Failure Rate of Small Businesses.* Entrepreneur. https://www.entrepreneur.com/starting-a-business/the-true-failure-rate-of-small-businesses/361350

Oxford English Press. (n.d.). Sunk Cost. In *Oxford English Dictionary.* Retrieved June 25, 2024, from https://www.oed.com/dictionary/sunk-cost_n?tab=meaning_and_use

Mazur, M., & Patterson, M. (Hosts). (2021-present). *Duped The Dark Side of Online Business* [Audio podcast]. Duped. https://duped.online/

Weekman, K. (2023, March 23). *Fitness-Turned-Christianity Influencer Brittany Dawn Just Addressed Her Upcoming Trial For The First Time*. BuzzFeed News. https://www.buzzfeednews.com/article/kelseyweekman/brittany-dawn-podcast-trial

Weekman, K. (2023, March 4). *The Trial Over Fitness-Turned-Christianity Influencer Brittany Dawn's Alleged Deceptive Business Practices Is Finally Starting. Here's Everything You Need To Know*. BuzzFeed News. https://www.buzzfeednews.com/article/kelseyweekman/influencer-brittany-dawn-trial-what-to-know

Lewis, M. (Host). (2022-2023). *Against the Rules* [Audio podcast]. Pushkin Industries. https://www.pushkin.fm/podcasts/against-the-rules

Mazur, M. (2023, May 3). *Make Marketing Suck Less*. Communication Rebel. https://drmichellemazur.com/2022/05/are-you-the-overlooked-expert.html

Garvin, D. A., & Margolis, J. D. (2015). *The Art of Giving and Receiving Advice*. Harvard Business Review. https://hbr.org/2015/01/the-art-of-giving-and-receiving-advice

Chapter 2:

Patterson, M. (2021). *How to Spot a Celebrity Entrepreneur*. BS-Free Business. https://bsfreebusiness.com/celebrity-entrepreneur-archetypes/

Campbell, A. (2024, June 13). *How to Scale a Business.* SCORE. https://www.score.org/resource/blog-post/how-scale-a-business

Harnish, V. (2022). *Scaling Up: How a Few Companies Make It... and Why the Rest Don't* (2nd ed.). ForbesBooks.

Dodson, D. (2022, October 3). *Why Do People Join Cults? Linguist and 'Cultish' Author Amanda Montell on the 'Invisible Power of Language'.* Parade. https://parade.com/1222232/dillondodson/amanda-montell-cultish-the-language-of-fanaticism-interview/

Hassan, S. (2023). *BITE Model of Authoritarian Control.* Freedom of Mind Resource Center. https://freedomofmind.com/cult-mind-control/bite-model-pdf-download/

Hooks, B. (2014). In *Feminist Theory: From Margin to Center* (3rd ed., pp. 84-95). Routledge. https://doi.org/10.4324/9781315743172

Mazur, M., & Patterson, M. (Hosts). (2023, December 11). The Fakery of Financial Feminism [Audio podcast episode]. In *Duped.* https://duped.online/2023/12/11/financial-feminism/

Patterson, M. (2022). *2022: The Year of the BS-Free Business.* BS-Free Business. https://bsfreebusiness.com/year-of-the-bs-free-business/

Patterson, M. (Host). (2023, May 1). The Realities of Burnout and Your Business with Brittany Berger [Audio podcast episode]. In *The BS-Free Service Business Show.* https://bsfreebusiness.com/realities-of-burnout/

Tsosie, R. (2014, August 25). *Indigenous Peoples and Sustainability Policy: Exploring the Politics and Practice of "Indigenous*

Sustainability". Global Institute of Sustainability and Innovation. https://sustainability-innovation.asu.edu/news/archive/indigenous-peoples-sustainability-policy-exploring-politics-practice-indigenous-sustainability/

United Nations. (1987, October). *Report of the World Commission on Environment and Development: Our Common Future.* Sustainable Development Goals Knowledge Platform. https://sustainabledevelopment.un.org/content/documents/5987our-common-future.pdf

Safdie, S. (2024, March 26). *What are the Three Pillars of Sustainable Development?* Greenly. https://greenly.earth/en-us/blog/company-guide/3-pillars-of-sustainable-development

Dudok van Heel, O. (2023, March 27). *Let's talk about 'regenerative business' not sustainability.* World Economic Forum. https://www.weforum.org/agenda/2023/03/regenerative-business-sustainability/

Chapter 3:

NeoMa Studios. (2023, October 4). *Why Do People Start Businesses in Every U.S. State?* Visual Capitalist. https://www.visualcapitalist.com/cp/why-do-people-start-businesses-every-us-state/

Main, K., & Bottorff, C. (2024, January 31). *Top Small Business Statistics of 2024.* Forbes Advisor. https://www.forbes.com/advisor/business/small-business-statistics/

Patterson, M. (n.d.). *Ditching Arbitrary Money Goals: Setting New Metrics for Personal Success.* BS-Free Business. https://bsfreebusiness.com/money-goals-2/

Patterson, M. (Host). (2021, May 3). The Basics of Capacity Planning [Audio podcast episode episode]. In *The BS-Free Service Business Show*. https://bsfreebusiness.com/capacity-planning/

Patterson, M. (Host). (2022, May 16). 7 Mistakes to Watch For When Selling Strategy [Audio podcast episode]. In *The BS-Free Service Business Show*. https://bsfreebusiness.com/selling-strategy/

Patterson, M. (n.d.). *Creatives, Coaches and Consultants: The Key Differences Between Different Types of Service Businesses*. BS-Free Business. https://bsfreebusiness.com/creatives-coaches-and-consultants/

Patterson, M. (Host). (2020, September 14). Masterminds: The Good, the Bad & the Ugly [Audio podcast episode]. In *The BS-Free Service Business Show*. https://bsfreebusiness.com/benefits-of-mastermind-groups/

Patterson, M. (Host). (2023, May 8). Sustainable Systems for Your Service Business [Audio podcast episode]. In *The BS-Free Service Business Show*. https://bsfreebusiness.com/sustainable-systems/

Chapter 4:

Patterson, M. (n.d.). *Small, Simple & Sustainable: The Profitable Service Business*. BS-Free Business. https://bsfreebusiness.com/profitable-service-business/

Patterson, M. (2020, April 20). *What I Learned About Investing in My Success By Spending $72,700*. BS-Free Business. https://bsfreebusiness.com/investing-in-my-success/

Cherry, K. (2024, May 21). *Social Comparison Theory in Psychology*. Verywell Mind. https://www.verywellmind.com/what-is-the-social-comparison-process-2795872

Wikimedia Foundation. (2024, November 20). *Keeping up with the Joneses (comics)*. Wikipedia. https://en.wikipedia.org/wiki/Keeping_Up_with_the_Joneses_(comics)

Wood, M. (2020, November 11). *What Is the Average Small Business Owner Salary?* Fundera. https://www.fundera.com/blog/study-finds-business-owners-earn-less

Murphy, S. (2023, September 15). *What Is Financial Trauma?* Shondaland. https://www.shondaland.com/live/money/a45103549/what-is-financial-trauma/

Chapter 5:

Patterson, M. (Host). (2023, May 1). The Realities of Burnout and Your Business with Brittany Berger [Audio podcast episode]. In *The BS-Free Service Business Show*. https://bsfreebusiness.com/realities-of-burnout/

Freeman, M. A., Johnson, S. L., Staudenmaier, P. J., & Zisser, M. R. (2015, April 17). *Are Entrepreneurs "Touched with Fire"? Pre-publication manuscript,* 1-34. https://michaelafreemanmd.com/Research_files/Are%20Entrepreneurs%20Touched%20with%20Fire%20(pre-pub%20n)%204-17-15.pdf

Mandel, C. (2021, August 30). *High rate of mental health conditions in women entrepreneurs "alarming," reports FLIK study*. BetaKit. https://betakit.com/high-rate-of-mental-health-conditions-in-women-entrepreneurs-alarming-reports-flik-study/

Ber Levtov, S. (n.d.). *Why Business Owners Should Care About Mental Health*. Shulamit Ber Levtov The Entrepreneur's Therapist. https://www.shula.ca/mental-health-entrepreneurship/

Work Brighter. (2021, December 22). *The 5 Stages of Hustle Culture Divestment*. Work Brighter. https://workbrighter.co/hustle-culture-divestment/

Patterson, M. (Host). (2021, May 3). The Basics of Capacity [Audio podcast episode]. In *The BS-Free Service Business Show*. https://bsfreebusiness.com/capacity-planning/

Patterson, M. (Host). (2021, June 14). Creating Time Freedom and Breaking Free from the Hustle with Becca Rich [Audio podcast episode]. In *The BS-Free Service Business Show*. https://bsfreebusiness.com/creating-time-freedom-and-breaking-free-from-the-hustle-with-becca-rich/

Canadian Federation of Independent Business. (2023, April 24). *The 8-day workweek: Small business owners clock in 59 hours a week to make up for labour shortages*. Cison. https://www.newswire.ca/news-releases/the-8-day-workweek-small-business-owners-clock-in-59-hours-a-week-to-make-up-for-labour-shortages-852635681.html

Xero. (2017, August 31). *Small Business Owners Are Nearly Four Times Less Likely to Disconnect on Vacation than the Average American Worker*. [Media release]. https://www.xero.com/content/dam/xero/pdf/media-release/xero-smb-vacation-survey-us-press-release.pdf

Pencavel, J. H. (2014, April 26). The Productivity of Working Hours. *IZA Institute of Labor Economics*, 1-57. https://dx.doi.org/10.2139/ssrn.2429648

Quaglia, S. (2020, February 11). *Experts reveal the ideal number of hours you should work each week.* Inverse. https://www.inverse.com/mind-body/how-many-hours-should-you-work-per-week

Patterson, M. (Host). (2023, April 24). How We Closed for 57 Days in 2022 [Audio podcast episode]. In *The BS-Free Service Business Show.* https://bsfreebusiness.com/closed-for-57-days/

Patterson, M. (Host). (2021, November 15). Hustle Culture and Ableism in Online Business With Brittany Berger [Audio podcast episode]. In *The BS-Free Service Business Show.* https://bsfreebusiness.com/ableism-in-online-business/

Patterson, M. (Host). (2024, April 15). Building a Business by Blending Products and Services with Zoe Linda [Audio podcast episode]. In *The BS-Free Service Business Show.* https://bsfreebusiness.com/products-and-services/

Beyondpsychhub. (2023, May 1). *What is Emotional Capacity, and How to Grow It in the Right Way?* Beyondpsychub. https://www.beyondpsychub.com/emotional-capacity/#google_vignette

Mental Health UK. (n.d.). *The stress bucket.* Mental Health UK. https://mentalhealth-uk.org/blog/the-stress-bucket/

Patterson, M. (Host). (2021, May 24). Sustainable Visibility* & Pitching Podcasts with Mai-kee Tsang [Audio podcast episode]. In *The BS-Free Service Business Show.* https://bsfreebusiness.com/sustainable-visibility/

Chapter 6:

Meyer, C., Muto, V., Jasper, M., Kussé, C., Lambot, E., Chellappa, S. L., Degueldre, C., Balteau, E., Luxen, A., Middleton, B., Archer, S. N., Collette, F., Dijk, D.-J., Phillips, C., Maquet, P., & Vandewalle, G. (2016, February 8). Seasonality in human cognitive brain responses. *PANS, 113*(11), 3066-3071. https://doi.org/10.1073/pnas.1518129113

Craft, L., & Fain, S. (2017, November 9). Ep. 26: Embrace Your Space— Decorate! (episode 26). In *Happier in Hollywood*. https://happierinhollywood.com/ep-26-embrace-your-space-decorate/

Moran, B., & Lennington, M. (2013). *The 12 Week Year*. John Wiley & Sons.

Chapter 7:

Fernet, C., Torrès, O., Austin, S., & St-Pierre, J. (2016, April 5). The psychological costs of owning and managing an SME: Linking job stressors, occupational loneliness, entrepreneurial orientation, and burnout. *Burnout research, 3*(2), 45-53. https://doi.org/10.1016/j.burn.2016.03.002

Weiss, R. S., & Bowlby, J. (1973). *Loneliness: the experience of emotional and social isolation*. MIT Press.

Ber Levtov, S. (n.d.). *7 Challenges to mental health for business owners*. Shulamit Ber Levtov The Entrepreneur's Therapist. https://www.shula.ca/entrepreneur-mental-health-7-challenges/

Freeman, M. A., Johnson, S. L., Staudenmaier, P. J., & Zisser, M. R. (2015, April 17). *Are Entrepreneurs "Touched with Fire"?* Pre-publication manuscript, 1-34. https://michaelafreemanmd.com/

Research_files/Are%20Entrepreneurs%20Touched%20with%20
Fire%20(pre-pub%20n)%204-17-15.pdf

Patterson, M. (n.d.). *Solo Business Owners: You're not playing small,
you're strategically small.* BS-Free Business. https://bsfreebusiness.
com/solo/

Patterson, M. (n.d.). *The 2023 Online Business Investment
Survey.* BS-Free Business. https://bsfreebusiness.
com/2023-online-business-investment-survey/

Chapter 8:

Patterson, M. (n.d.). *Staying Solo: Your Framework for a Simple
Sustainable Service Business.* BS-Free Business. https://
bsfreebusiness.com/staying-solo/

Oxford English Press. (n.d.). System. In *Oxford English Dictionary.*
Retrieved June 25, 2024, from https://www.oed.com/dictionary/
system_n?tab=meaning_and_use

Patterson, M. (n.d.). *Staying Solo: Carving Out Consistent
Space.* BS-Free Business. https://bsfreebusiness.com/
staying-solo-by-creating-space/

Patterson, M. (2019, December 8). *Where Sales and Marketing Advice
Can Go Seriously Wrong.* BS-Free Business. https://bsfreebusiness.
com/bad-sales-advice/

Patterson, M. (2020, April 20). *What I Learned About Investing in
My Success By Spending $72,700.* BS-Free Business. https://
bsfreebusiness.com/investing-in-my-success/

Johnson, J. (2020, July 7). *What is decision fatigue?* Medical News Today. https://www.medicalnewstoday.com/articles/decision-fatigue

Patterson, M. (2022, September 5). *BS-Free Sustainability for Service Businesses.* BS-Free Business. https://bsfreebusiness.com/sustainability-for-service-business/

Puthiyamadam, T., & Reyes, J. (2018). *Experience is everything: Here's how to get it right.* PwC. https://www.pwc.com/us/en/services/consulting/library/consumer-intelligence-series/future-of-customer-experience.html

Gallo, A. (2014, October 29). *The Value of Keeping the Right Customers.* Harvard Business Review. https://hbr.org/2014/10/the-value-of-keeping-the-right-customers

Chapter 9:

Coursera Staff. (2024, December 10). *The 4 Ps of Marketing: What They Are and How to Use Them.* Coursera. https://www.coursera.org/articles/4-ps-of-marketing

Patterson, M. (2022, May 2). *VIP Days and Retainers: What's Right For You?* BS-Free Business. https://bsfreebusiness.com/vip-days-and-retainers/

Patterson, M. (2023, March 27). *The Power of Retainer Clients.* BS-Free Business. https://bsfreebusiness.com/retainer-clients/

Patterson, M. (2023, March 20). *Should You Offer VIP Day Services?* BS-Free Business. https://bsfreebusiness.com/vip-days/

Chapter 10:

Rogers, S., Cook, J., & Pieters, L. (2022, May 20). *When rising prices break consumers' trust*. Deloitte Insights. https://www2.deloitte.com/xe/en/insights/industry/retail-distribution/consumer-behavior-trends-state-of-the-consumer-tracker/price-gouging-and-rising-us-inflation.html

PwC. (n.d.). 2022 Trust Consumer Intelligence Series. PwC. Retrieved June 24, 2024, from https://www.pwc.com/us/en/services/consulting/library/consumer-intelligence-series/trust-new-business-currency.html

Anderson, E. T., & Simester, D. I. (2008, January). Price Cues and Customer Price Knowledge. 1-28. https://www.kellogg.northwestern.edu/faculty/anderson_e/htm/personalpage_files/Papers/Price%20Cues%20Book%20Chapter%20Jan%203.pdf

Anderson, E. T., & Simester, D. I. (2003, September). *Mind Your Pricing Cues*. Harvard Business Review. https://hbr.org/2003/09/mind-your-pricing-cues

Klontz, B., Britt, S. L., Mentzer, J., & Klontz, T. (2011). Money Beliefs and Financial Behaviors: Development of the Klontz Money Script Inventory. *The Journal of Financial Therapy, 2*(1). doi.org/10.4148/jft.v2i1.451

Chapter 11:

Gertenbach, E. (n.d.). *Stress-Free SEO Strategy*. EG Creative Content. https://www.egcreativecontent.com/b2b-seo-content-strategy

Chapter 12:

Patterson, M. (Host). (2024, April 1). From Solo to Agency and Back Again with Jules Taggart [Audio podcast episode]. In *The BS-Free Service Business Show*. https://bsfreebusiness.com/solo-to-agency/

Patterson, M. (2021, October 11). *The Agency Business Model: Is it Right For You?* BS-Free Business. https://bsfreebusiness.com/the-agency-business-model-is-it-right-for-you/

Nelson, N. (2023, September 5). *What is a micro business?.* Wolters Kluwer. https://www.wolterskluwer.com/en/expert-insights/what-is-a-micro-business

SoDA & Productive. (2022, February 11). *The Global Agency Landscape 2022 Report*. Productive. https://productive.io/the-global-agency-landscape-2022-report/

If you're a solo business owner who's intrigued by the agency business model as a possibility for your business, I encourage you to check out my podcast *Confessions of a Micro Agency Owner* where we talk about all of this. You can find it on Apple Podcasts, Spotify or wherever you get your podcasts.

Chapter 13:

Patterson, M. (2023, May 15). Sustainable Systems: Tame the Client Service Chaos. *BS-Free Business*. https://bsfreebusiness.com/client-service-chaos/

Patterson, M. (2023, November 8). Three Tips to Better Manage Client Expectations. *BS-Free Business*. https://bsfreebusiness.com/manage-client-expectations/

Acknowledgements

Sending so much gratitude for you picking up and reading this book. I also want to thank all the wonderful humans who made getting this book out into the world possible.

For their kick in the ass and ongoing encouragement, my friends Jules Taggart and Megan Flatt. They told me it was time to write the book, and it turns out they were right.

My sister, bestie, hype squad, and world's best co-worker, Sara Freeburn — you helped me make space for this project, and as the first reader promised to tell me the truth. Everyone needs a Sara.

Special thanks to my editor, Kris Emery, for whipping my drafts into shape and adding great context as you know me and my message so well.

Big props to Ella Freeburn and Isabel Dukes for their work with citations, approvals, and all the other details that were needed to ensure this book is legit.

Jessica Suhr and the team at Perennial Creative for the book's cover design and all of the graphics on this project. You've made me look amazing for years, and this project is no exception.

Sarah Bones, thank you for your careful proofreading and catching all the things that would have annoyed me once the book was published.

Sending a big old hat tip to all of my early readers who provided great input that helped me feel confident in the final product, as well as the countless individuals who shared the stories and quotes used in this book.

Last but not least, my kid who's the reason I ended up on this journey in the first place. And my husband who has never ever doubted for a minute that I'd make working for myself work, and never ever questioned what I was doing when I was "working on my book" while watching reality TV.

About the Author

Maggie Patterson is the creator of BS-Free Business which focuses on consulting and support for service-based business owners. She has spent her entire career in client services, first as a PR professional in a fast-growing agency, and then as an entrepreneur who's had multiple successful businesses over the past 20 years.

Today, Maggie is a vocal advocate for solo and microbusiness owners who want to right-size their businesses and have a life away from work. She works hands-on with service business owners every single day on everything shared in this book. Plus, she works with mid-size corporate clients on content and communications strategy, hosts multiple podcasts, and is always writing something. (Next up: A fiction project!)

When she's not working, writing or podcasting, she's outside enjoying three of the four Canadian seasons, hanging with her husband, kid or friends, or hiding out with a book not talking to anyone.